THE YALE SHAKESPEARE

Edited by

Wilbur L. Cross   Tucker Brooke

Published under the Direction
of the
Department of English, Yale University,
on the Fund
Given to the Yale University Press in 1917
by the Members of the
Kingsley Trust Association
(Scroll and Key Society of Yale College)
To Commemorate the Seventy-Fifth Anniversary
of the Founding of the Society

·: The Yale Shakespeare :·

THE THIRD PART OF
KING HENRY THE SIXTH

EDITED BY

TUCKER BROOKE

NEW HAVEN · YALE UNIVERSITY PRESS
LONDON · HUMPHREY MILFORD
OXFORD UNIVERSITY PRESS · MCMXXIII

PRINTED IN THE UNITED STATES OF AMERICA

TABLE OF CONTENTS

The facsimile opposite reproduces the title-page of the Elizabethan Club copy of Thomas Pavier's (1619) edition of the two plays upon which the second and third parts of 'King Henry VI' were based. Shakespeare's name is here for the first time connected with them

THE
Whole Contention

betweene the two Famous
Houses, LANCASTER and
YORKE.

With the Tragicall ends of the good Duke
Humfrey, Richard Duke of Yorke,
and King Henrie the
sixt.

Diuided into two Parts : And newly corrected and
enlarged. Written by *William Shake-*
speare, Gent.

Printed at LONDON, for T. P.

[DRAMATIS PERSONÆ

KING HENRY THE SIXTH
EDWARD, PRINCE OF WALES, *his Son*
LOUIS THE ELEVENTH, *King of France*
DUKE OF SOMERSET
DUKE OF EXETER
EARL OF NORTHUMBERLAND
EARL OF OXFORD   *Lancastrians*
EARL OF WESTMORELAND
HENRY, EARL OF RICHMOND, *a Boy*
LORD CLIFFORD
RICHARD PLANTAGENET, DUKE OF YORK
EDWARD, EARL OF MARCH, *later King Edward IV*
EDMUND, EARL OF RUTLAND
GEORGE, *later Duke of Clarence*   *his Sons*
RICHARD, *later Duke of Gloucester*
DUKE OF NORFOLK
MARQUESS OF MONTAGUE
EARL OF WARWICK
EARL OF PEMBROKE
LORD HASTINGS   *Yorkists*
LORD STAFFORD
SIR JOHN MORTIMER } *Uncles to the Duke of York*
SIR HUGH MORTIMER
LORD RIVERS, *Brother to Lady Grey*
SIR JOHN MONTGOMERY } *Followers of King Edward IV*
SIR WILLIAM STANLEY
SIR JOHN SOMERVILLE, *a Follower of Warwick*
A Nobleman, *bearing a message*
ROBERT ASPALL, *Tutor to Rutland*
Lieutenant of the Tower
Mayor of York
Two Gamekeepers
A Huntsman
A Son that has killed his Father
A Father that has killed his Son

MARGARET OF ANJOU, *Queen to King Henry*
LADY GREY, *later Queen to King Edward*
LADY BONA, *Sister to the French Queen*
A Nurse, *with the infant son of King Edward*
Soldiers, Attendants, Messengers, Watchmen, *etc.*

SCENE: *London and Westminster, Paris, York, Coventry, and Chipping Norton; Sandal Castle in Yorkshire; Battle-fields of Wakefield, Towton, Barnet, and Tewkesbury; Open Country in England.*]

The Third Part of Henry the Sixth, with the Death of the Duke of York

ACT FIRST

Scene One

[*London.   The Parliament-House*]

Alarum.   Enter Plantagenet, Edward, Richard, Norfolk, Montague, Warwick, and Soldiers.

War. I wonder how the king escap'd our hands.
  York. While we pursu'd the horsemen of the north,
He slily stole away and left his men:
Whereat the great Lord of Northumberland,   4
Whose warlike ears could never brook retreat,
Cheer'd up the drooping army; and himself,
Lord Clifford, and Lord Stafford, all abreast,
Charg'd our main battle's front, and breaking in   8
Were by the swords of common soldiers slain.
  Edw. Lord Stafford's father, Duke of Buckingham,
Is either slain or wounded dangerous;
I cleft his beaver with a downright blow: 12
That this is true, father, behold his blood.
                [*Showing his bloody sword.*]
  Mont. And, brother, here's the Earl of Wiltshire's blood,
Whom I encounter'd as the battles join'd.
  Rich. Speak thou for me, and tell them what I did. 16
    [*Throwing down the Duke of Somerset's head.*]

Scene One. S. d. Plantagenet; *cf. n.*   1 *Cf. n.*
5 retreat: *trumpet-call commanding retirement*
7 Lord Clifford; *cf. n.*   12 beaver: *face-guard of helmet*
14 brother; *cf. n.*

York. Richard hath best deserv'd of all my sons.
But is your Grace dead, my Lord of Somerset?

   Norf. Such hope have all the line of John of Gaunt!

   Rich. Thus do I hope to shake King Henry's head. 20

   War. And so do I.   Victorious Prince of York,
Before I see thee seated in that throne
Which now the house of Lancaster usurps,
I vow by heaven these eyes shall never close.   24
This is the palace of the fearful king,
And this the regal seat: possess it, York;
For this is thine, and not King Henry's heirs'.

   York. Assist me, then, sweet Warwick, and I
     will;   28
For hither we have broken in by force.

   Norf. We'll all assist you; he that flies shall die.

   York. Thanks, gentle Norfolk.   Stay by me, my
     lords;
And, soldiers, stay and lodge by me this night.   32
                              They go up.

   War. And when the king comes, offer him no
     violence,
Unless he seek to thrust you out perforce.
                       [The Soldiers retire.]

   York. The queen this day here holds her parliament,
But little thinks we shall be of her council: 36
By words or blows here let us win our right.

   Rich. Arm'd as we are, let's stay within this house.

   War. The bloody parliament shall this be call'd,
Unless Plantagenet, Duke of York, be king,   40
And bashful Henry depos'd, whose cowardice
Hath made us by-words to our enemies.

   York. Then leave me not, my lords; be resolute;

17 *Cf. n.*
19 *May all the descendants of John of Gaunt expect the same*
32 *S. d.* They go up; *cf. n.*   35 *Cf. n.*

I mean to take possession of my right.   44

   War. Neither the king, nor he that loves him best,
The proudest he that holds up Lancaster,
Dares stir a wing if Warwick shake his bells.
I'll plant Plantagenet, root him up who dares.   48
Resolve thee, Richard; claim the English crown.
[*Warwick leads York to the throne, who seats himself.*]

*Flourish.   Enter King Henry, Clifford, Northumber-
      land, Westmoreland, Exeter, and the rest.*

   Henry. My lords, look where the sturdy rebel sits,
Even in the chair of state! belike he means—
Back'd by the power of Warwick, that false peer— 52
To aspire unto the crown and reign as king.
Earl of Northumberland, he slew thy father,
And thine, Lord Clifford; and you both have vow'd
      revenge
On him, his sons, his favourites, and his friends.   56
   North. If I be not, heavens be reveng'd on me!
   Clif. The hope thereof makes Clifford mourn in
      steel.
   West. What! shall we suffer this? let's pluck him
      down:
My heart for anger burns; I cannot brook it.   60
   Henry. Be patient, gentle Earl of Westmoreland.
   Clif. Patience is for poltroons, such as he:
He durst not sit there had your father liv'd.
My gracious lord, here in the parliament   64
Let us assail the family of York.
   North. Well hast thou spoken, cousin: be it so.
   Henry. Ah! know you not the city favours them,
And they have troops of soldiers at their beck?   68

---

46 he: *man*   holds up: *supports the cause of*
47 shake his bells; *cf. n.*   49 Resolve thee: *be resolute*
57 be not: *be not revenged*   67 the city favours them; *cf. n.*

Exe. But when the duke is slain, they'll quickly fly.

Henry. Far be the thought of this from Henry's heart,

To make a shambles of the parliament-house!

Cousin of Exeter, frowns, words, and threats   72

Shall be the war that Henry means to use.

Thou factious Duke of York, descend my throne,

And kneel for grace and mercy at my feet;

I am thy sovereign.

    York.   I am thine.   76

    Exe. For shame! come down: he made thee Duke of York.

    York. It was my inheritance, as the earldom was.

    Exe. Thy father was a traitor to the crown.

    War. Exeter, thou art a traitor to the crown   80

In following this usurping Henry.

    Clif. Whom should he follow but his natural king?

    War. True, Clifford; that is Richard, Duke of York.

    Henry. And shall I stand, and thou sit in my throne?   84

    York. It must and shall be so: content thyself.

    War. Be Duke of Lancaster: let him be king.

    West. He is both king and Duke of Lancaster;

And that the Lord of Westmoreland shall maintain. 88

    War. And Warwick shall disprove it. You forget

That we are those which chas'd you from the field

And slew your fathers, and with colours spread

March'd through the city to the palace gates.   92

    North. Yes, Warwick, I remember it to my grief;

And, by his soul, thou and thy house shall rue it.

    West. Plantagenet, of thee, and these thy sons,

Thy kinsmen and thy friends, I'll have more lives 96

Than drops of blood were in my father's veins.

78 earldom: *of March*   79 *Cf. n.*
88 Lord of Westmoreland; *cf. n.*

Clif. Urge it no more; lest that instead of words
I send thee, Warwick, such a messenger
As shall revenge his death before I stir.   100
    War. Poor Clifford! how I scorn his worthless
       threats.
    York. Will you we show our title to the crown?
If not, our swords shall plead it in the field.   103
    Henry. What title hast thou, traitor, to the crown?
Thy father was, as thou art, Duke of York;
Thy grandfather, Roger Mortimer, Earl of March;
I am the son of Henry the Fifth,
Who made the Dauphin and the French to stoop,   108
And seiz'd upon their towns and provinces.
    War. Talk not of France, sith thou hast lost it all.
    Henry. The Lord Protector lost it, and not I:
When I was crown'd I was but nine months old.   112
    Rich. You are old enough now, and yet, methinks,
       you lose.
Father, tear the crown from the usurper's head.
    Edw. Sweet father, do so; set it on your head.
    Mont. [*To York.*] Good brother, as thou lov'st and
       honour'st arms,   116
Let's fight it out and not stand cavilling thus.
    Rich. Sound drums and trumpets, and the king will
       fly.
    York. Sons, peace!
    Henry. Peace thou! and give King Henry leave to
       speak.   120
    War. Plantagenet shall speak first: hear him, lords;
And be you silent and attentive too,
For he that interrupts him shall not live.
    Henry. Think'st thou that I will leave my kingly
       throne,   124

105 *Cf. n.*   106 Thy grandfather: *on the mother's side*
110 sith: *since*   113 old enough now: *i.e. thirty-nine years old*

Wherein my grandsire and my father sat?
No: first shall war unpeople this my realm;
Ay, and their colours, often borne in France,
And now in England to our heart's great sorrow,   128
Shall be my winding-sheet.   Why faint you, lords?
My title's good, and better far than his.

    War. Prove it, Henry, and thou shalt be king.

    Henry. Henry the Fourth by conquest got the
    crown.   132

    York. 'Twas by rebellion against his king.

    Henry. [*Aside.*] I know not what to say: my title's
    weak.

[*Aloud.*] Tell me, may not a king adopt an heir?

    York. What then?   136

    Henry. An if he may, then am I lawful king;
For Richard, in the view of many lords,
Resign'd the crown to Henry the Fourth,
Whose heir my father was, and I am his.   140

    York. He rose against him, being his sovereign,
And made him to resign his crown perforce.

    War. Suppose, my lords, he did it unconstrain'd,
Think you 'twere prejudicial to his crown?   144

    Exe. No; for he could not so resign his crown
But that the next heir should succeed and reign.

    Henry. Art thou against us, Duke of Exeter?

    Exe. His is the right, and therefore pardon me. 148

    York. Why whisper you, my lords, and answer not?

    Exe. My conscience tells me he is lawful king.

    Henry. [*Aside.*] All will revolt from me, and turn
    to him.

    North. Plantagenet, for all the claim thou lay'st, 152
Think not that Henry shall be so depos'd.

    War. Depos'd he shall be in despite of all.

144 crown: *legal claim to the crown*

North. Thou art deceiv'd: 'tis not thy southern
    power,
Of Essex, Norfolk, Suffolk, nor of Kent,   156
Which makes thee thus presumptuous and proud,
Can set the duke up in despite of me.

    Clif. King Henry, be thy title right or wrong,
Lord Clifford vows to fight in thy defence: 160
May that ground gape and swallow me alive,
Where I shall kneel to him that slew my father!

    Henry. O Clifford, how thy words revive my heart!

    York. Henry of Lancaster, resign thy crown.   164
What mutter you, or what conspire you, lords?

    War. Do right unto this princely Duke of York,
Or I will fill the house with armed men,
And o'er the chair of state, where now he sits,   168
Write up his title with usurping blood.

       He stamps with his foot, and the Soldiers show
                  themselves.

    Henry. My Lord of Warwick, hear me but one
    word:—
Let me for this my life-time reign as king.

    York. Confirm the crown to me and to mine heirs, 172
And thou shalt reign in quiet while thou liv'st.

    Henry. I am content: Richard Plantagenet,
Enjoy the kingdom after my decease.

    Clif. What wrong is this unto the prince your
    son!   176

    War. What good is this to England and himself!

    West. Base, fearful, and despairing Henry!

    Clif. How hast thou injur'd both thyself and us!

    West. I cannot stay to hear these articles.   180

    North. Nor I.

    Clif. Come, cousin, let us tell the queen these news.

155 deceiv'd: *mistaken*   thou thy southern power; *cf. n.*
158 Can: *that can*

West. Farewell, faint-hearted and degenerate king,
In whose cold blood no spark of honour bides.   184

North. Be thou a prey unto the house of York,
And die in bands for this unmanly deed!

Clif. In dreadful war mayst thou be overcome,
Or live in peace abandon'd and despis'd!   188

> [*Exeunt Northumberland, Clifford, and West-*
> *moreland.*]

War. Turn this way, Henry, and regard them not.

Exe. They seek revenge and therefore will not yield.

Henry. Ah! Exeter.

War.   Why should you sigh, my lord?

Henry. Not for myself, Lord Warwick, but my
    son,   192
Whom I unnaturally shall disinherit.
But be it as it may; I here entail
The crown to thee and to thine heirs for ever;
Conditionally, that here thou take an oath   196
To cease this civil war, and, whilst I live,
To honour me as thy king and sovereign;
And neither by treason nor hostility
To seek to put me down and reign thyself.   200

York. This oath I willingly take and will perform.
> [*Coming from the throne.*]

War. Long live King Henry! Plantagenet, em-
    brace him.

Henry. And long live thou and these thy forward
    sons!

York. Now York and Lancaster are reconcil'd.   204

Exe. Accurs'd be he that seeks to make them foes!
> *Sennet. Here they come down.*

York. Farewell, my gracious lord; I'll to my castle.

---

186 bands: *bonds*
205 S. d. Sennet: *bugle notes to signal the moving of a procession*
206 castle: *Sandal Castle, near Wakefield (Yorkshire)*

War. And I'll keep London with my soldiers.

Norf. And I to Norfolk with my followers. 208

Mont. And I unto the sea from whence I came.

[*Exeunt York and his Sons, Warwick, Norfolk,*
Montague, Soldiers, and Attendants.]

Henry. And I, with grief and sorrow, to the court.

Enter the Queen [and the Prince of Wales].

Exe. Here comes the queen, whose looks bewray her
    anger: 211

I'll steal away. [*Going.*]

  Henry.   Exeter, so will I. [*Going.*]

  Queen. Nay, go not from me; I will follow thee.

  Henry. Be patient, gentle queen, and I will stay.

  Queen. Who can be patient in such extremes?

Ah! wretched man; would I had died a maid, 216

And never seen thee, never borne thee son,

Seeing thou hast prov'd so unnatural a father.

Hath he deserv'd to lose his birthright thus?

Hadst thou but lov'd him half so well as I, 220

Or felt that pain which I did for him once,

Or nourish'd him as I did with my blood,

Thou wouldst have left thy dearest heart-blood there,

Rather than have made that savage duke thine
    heir, 224

And disinherited thine only son.

  Prince. Father, you cannot disinherit me:

If you be king, why should not I succeed?

  Henry. Pardon me, Margaret; pardon me, sweet
    son; 228

The Earl of Warwick and the duke enforc'd me.

  Queen. Enforc'd thee! art thou king, and wilt be
    forc'd?

I shame to hear thee speak. Ah! timorous wretch;

209 unto the sea; *cf. n.*   211 bewray: *disclose*   226 *Cf. n.*

Thou hast undone thyself, thy son, and me;   232
And given unto the house of York such head
As thou shalt reign but by their sufferance.
To entail him and his heirs unto the crown,
What is it but to make thy sepulchre,   236
And creep into it far before thy time?
Warwick is chancellor and the Lord of Calais;
Stern Faulconbridge commands the narrow seas;
The duke is made protector of the realm;   240
And yet shalt thou be safe? such safety finds
The trembling lamb environed with wolves.
Had I been there, which am a silly woman,
The soldiers should have toss'd me on their pikes   244
Before I would have granted to that act;
But thou preferr'st thy life before thine honour:
And seeing thou dost, I here divorce myself,
Both from thy table, Henry, and thy bed,   248
Until that act of parliament be repeal'd
Whereby my son is disinherited.
The northern lords that have forsworn thy colours
Will follow mine, if once they see them spread;   252
And spread they shall be, to thy foul disgrace,
And utter ruin of the house of York.
Thus do I leave thee. Come, son, let's away;
Our army is ready; come, we'll after them.   256
    Henry. Stay, gentle Margaret, and hear me speak.
    Queen. Thou hast spoke too much already: get thee
       gone.
    Henry. Gentle son Edward, thou wilt stay with me?
    Queen. Ay, to be murther'd by his enemies.   260
    Prince. When I return with victory from the field
I'll see your Grace: till then, I'll follow her.

233 head: *headway*   239 *Cf. n.*   narrow seas: *English Channel*
243 which: *who*   silly: *feeble*   245 granted: *submitted*

Queen. Come, son, away; we may not linger thus.
                    [*Exeunt Queen and the Prince.*]
Henry. Poor queen! how love to me and to her
  son   264
Hath made her break out into terms of rage.
Reveng'd may she be on that hateful duke,
Whose haughty spirit, winged with desire,
Will cost my crown, and like an empty eagle   268
Tire on the flesh of me and of my son!
The loss of those three lords torments my heart:
I'll write unto them, and entreat them fair.
Come, cousin; you shall be the messenger.   272
  Exe. And I, I hope, shall reconcile them all.
                              Exit [*with Henry*].

Scene Two

[*A Room in Sandal Castle, near Wakefield, in
Yorkshire*]

Flourish.   Enter Richard, Edward, and Montague.

Rich. Brother, though I be youngest, give me leave.
Edw. No, I can better play the orator.
Mont. But I have reasons strong and forcible.

Enter the Duke of York.

York. Why, how now, sons and brother! at a
  strife?   4
What is your quarrel? how began it first?
  Edw. No quarrel, but a slight contention.
  York. About what?
  Rich. About that which concerns your Grace and
  us: 8

268 cost: *assail*   empty: *famished*   269 Tire: *gorge*
271 entreat . . . fair: *propitiate them*
1 give me leave: *let me speak*

The crown of England, father, which is yours.

 York. Mine, boy? not till King Henry be dead.

 Rich. Your right depends not on his life or death.

 Edw. Now you are heir, therefore enjoy it now: 12
By giving the house of Lancaster leave to breathe,
It will outrun you, father, in the end.

 York. I took an oath that he should quietly reign.

 Edw. But for a kingdom any oath may be broken: 16
I would break a thousand oaths to reign one year.

 Rich. No; God forbid your Grace should be forsworn.

 York. I shall be, if I claim by open war.

 Rich. I'll prove the contrary, if you'll hear me
 speak.
                20

 York. Thou canst not, son; it is impossible.

 Rich. An oath is of no moment, being not took
Before a true and lawful magistrate
That hath authority over him that swears: 24
Henry had none, but did usurp the place;
Then, seeing 'twas he that made you to depose,
Your oath, my lord, is vain and frivolous.
Therefore, to arms! And, father, do but think 28
How sweet a thing it is to wear a crown,
Within whose circuit is Elysium,
And all that poets feign of bliss and joy.
Why do we linger thus? I cannot rest   32
Until the white rose that I wear be dy'd
Even in the lukewarm blood of Henry's heart.

 York. Richard, enough, I will be king, or die.
Brother, thou shalt to London presently,   36
And whet on Warwick to this enterprise.
Thou, Richard, shalt to the Duke of Norfolk,
And tell him privily of our intent.

---

22 moment: *weight*   26 made . . . depose: *administered the oath*
28-31 *Cf. n.*   36 presently: *at once*

You, Edward, shall unto my Lord Cobham,   40
With whom the Kentishmen will willingly rise:
In them I trust; for they are soldiers,
Witty, courteous, liberal, full of spirit.
While you are thus employ'd, what resteth more,   44
But that I seek occasion how to rise,
And yet the king not privy to my drift,
Nor any of the house of Lancaster?

Enter Gabriel [a Messenger].

But, stay: what news? why com'st thou in such post? 48
   Mess. The queen with all the northern earls and
     lords
Intend here to besiege you in your castle.
She is hard by with twenty thousand men,
And therefore fortify your hold, my lord.   52
   York. Ay, with my sword. What! think'st thou that
     we fear them?
Edward and Richard, you shall stay with me;
My brother Montague shall post to London:
Let noble Warwick, Cobham, and the rest,   56
Whom we have left protectors of the king,
With powerful policy strengthen themselves,
And trust not simple Henry nor his oaths.
   Mont. Brother, I go; I'll win them, fear it not: 60
And thus most humbly I do take my leave.

                  Exit Montague.

Enter Mortimer, and his Brother.

   York. Sir John, and Sir Hugh Mortimer, mine
     uncles!

42, 43 *Cf. n.*   43 Witty: *wise*   liberal: *gentlemanly*
44 resteth: *remains to be done*
46 privy . . . drift: *aware of my intention*
47 S. d. Gabriel; *cf. n.*   48 post: *haste*   52 hold: *castle*
58 powerful policy: *cunningly-gained power*

You are come to Sandal in a happy hour;
The army of the queen mean to besiege us.   64

 Sir John. She shall not need, we'll meet her in the field.

 York. What! with five thousand men?

 Rich. Ay, with five hundred, father, for a need:
A woman's general; what should we fear?   68

          A march afar off.

 Edw. I hear their drums; let's set our men in order,
And issue forth and bid them battle straight.

 York. Five men to twenty! though the odds be great,
I doubt not, uncle, of our victory.   72
Many a battle have I won in France,
When as the enemy hath been ten to one:
Why should I not now have the like success?

         Alarum.   Exeunt.

Scene Three

[Field of Battle between Sandal Castle and Wakefield]

Enter Rutland, and his Tutor.

 Rut. Ah, whither shall I fly to 'scape their hands?
Ah! tutor, look, where bloody Clifford comes!

Enter Clifford [and Soldiers].

 Clif. Chaplain, away! thy priesthood saves thy life.
As for the brat of this accursed duke,   4
Whose father slew my father, he shall die.

 Tut. And I, my lord, will bear him company.

 Clif. Soldiers, away with him.

 Tut. Ah! Clifford, murther not this innocent child, 8
Lest thou be hated both of God and man!

      Exit [forced off by Soldiers].

75 the like: *equal*

Clif. How now! is he dead already? Or is it fear
That makes him close his eyes? I'll open them.

Rut. So looks the pent-up lion o'er the wretch   12
That trembles under his devouring paws;
And so he walks, insulting o'er his prey,
And so he comes to rend his limbs asunder.
Ah! gentle Clifford, kill me with thy sword,   16
And not with such a cruel threatening look.
Sweet Clifford! hear me speak before I die:
I am too mean a subject for thy wrath;
Be thou reveng'd on men, and let me live.   20

Clif. In vain thou speak'st, poor boy; my father's
          blood
Hath stopp'd the passage where thy words should
          enter.

Rut. Then let my father's blood open it again:
He is a man, and, Clifford, cope with him.   24

Clif. Had I thy brethren here, their lives and thine
Were not revenge sufficient for me;
No, if I digg'd up thy forefathers' graves,
And hung their rotten coffins up in chains,   28
It could not slake mine ire, nor ease my heart.
The sight of any of the house of York
Is as a fury to torment my soul;
And till I root out their accursed line,   32
And leave not one alive, I live in hell.
Therefore—   [*Lifting his hand.*]

Rut. O! let me pray before I take my death.
To thee I pray; sweet Clifford, pity me!   36

Clif. Such pity as my rapier's point affords.

Rut. I never did thee harm: why wilt thou slay me?

Clif. Thy father hath.

Rut.   But 'twas ere I was born.

---

12 pent-up: *caged, rendered fierce*
14 insulting: *exulting in triumph*   39 ere I was born; *cf. n.*

Thou hast one son; for his sake pity me,   40
Lest in revenge thereof, sith God is just,
He be as miserably slain as I.
Ah! let me live in prison all my days;
And when I give occasion of offence,   44
Then let me die, for now thou hast no cause.
    Clif. No cause!
Thy father slew my father; therefore, die.
                          [Stabs him.]
    Rut. Dii faciant laudis summa sit ista tuæ! *[Dies.]*
    Clif. Plantagenet! I come, Plantagenet!
And this thy son's blood cleaving to my blade
Shall rust upon my weapon, till thy blood,
Congeal'd with this, do make me wipe off both.   *Exit.*

Scene Four

[Another Part of the Plains]

Alarum. Enter Richard, Duke of York.

    York. The army of the queen hath got the field:
My uncles both are slain in rescuing me;
And all my followers to the eager foe
Turn back and fly, like ships before the wind,   4
Or lambs pursu'd by hunger-starved wolves.
My sons, God knows what hath bechanced them:
But this I know, they have demean'd themselves
Like men born to renown by life or death.   8
Three times did Richard make a lane to me,
And thrice cried, 'Courage, father! fight it out!'
And full as oft came Edward to my side,
With purple falchion, painted to the hilt   12

48 *'The gods grant that this be the height of thy glory'*
4 Turn back: *present their backs*   7 demean'd: *behaved*
12 purple: *blood-color*   falchion: *curved sword, sabre*

In blood of those that had encounter'd him:
And when the hardiest warriors did retire,
Richard cried, 'Charge! and give no foot of ground!'
And cried, 'A crown, or else a glorious tomb!   16
A sceptre, or an earthly sepulchre!'
With this, we charg'd again; but, out, alas!
We bodg'd again: as I have seen a swan
With bootless labour swim against the tide,   20
And spend her strength with over-matching waves.

                              A short alarum within.

Ah, hark! the fatal followers do pursue;
And I am faint and cannot fly their fury;
And were I strong I would not shun their fury: 24
The sands are number'd that makes up my life;
Here must I stay, and here my life must end.

*Enter the Queen, Clifford, Northumberland, the young
            Prince, and Soldiers.*

Come, bloody Clifford, rough Northumberland,
I dare your quenchless fury to more rage: 28
I am your butt, and I abide your shot.
    North. Yield to our mercy, proud Plantagenet.
    Clif. Ay, to such mercy as his ruthless arm
With downright payment show'd unto my father.   32
Now Phaethon hath tumbled from his car,
And made an evening at the noontide prick.
    York. My ashes, as the phœnix, may bring forth
A bird that will revenge upon you all;   36
And in that hope I throw mine eyes to heaven,
Scorning whate'er you can afflict me with.
Why come you not? what! multitudes, and fear?
    Clif. So cowards fight when they can fly no further;

19 bodg'd: *gave way*   21 with: *against*   25 makes; *cf. n.*
29 butt: *mark at archery*   33 Phaethon; *cf. n.*
34 noontide prick: *midday mark on the sundial*

So doves do peck the falcon's piercing talons;
So desperate thieves, all hopeless of their lives,
Breathe out invectives 'gainst the officers.

   York. O Clifford! but bethink thee once again,   44
And in thy thought o'er-run my former time;
And, if thou canst for blushing, view this face,
And bite thy tongue, that slanders him with cowardice
Whose frown hath made thee faint and fly ere this.   48

   Clif. I will not bandy with thee word for word,
But buckle with thee blows, twice two for one.

   Queen. Hold, valiant Clifford! for a thousand causes
I would prolong awhile the traitor's life.   52
Wrath makes him deaf: speak thou, Northumberland.

   North. Hold, Clifford! do not honour him so much
To prick thy finger, though to wound his heart.
What valour were it, when a cur doth grin,   56
For one to thrust his hand between his teeth,
When he might spurn him with his foot away?
It is war's prize to take all vantages,
And ten to one is no impeach of valour.   60

         [They lay hands on York, who struggles.]

   Clif. Ay, ay; so strives the woodcock with the gin.

   North. So doth the cony struggle in the net.

   York. So triumph thieves upon their conquer'd
      booty;
So true men yield, with robbers so o'er-matched.   64

   North. What would your Grace have done unto him
      now?

   Queen. Brave warriors, Clifford and Northumber-
      land,
Come, make him stand upon this molehill here,

---

45 o'er-run: *review*   50 buckle . . . blows: *strive with blows*
56 grin: *show his teeth*   59 prize: *privilege*
60 impeach: *derogation*
61 woodcock: *a proverbially silly bird*   gin: *snare*
62 cony: *rabbit*
                                       67 *Cf. n.*

That raught at mountains with outstretched arms,   68
Yet parted but the shadow with his hand.
What! was it you that would be England's king?
Was 't you that revell'd in our parliament,
And made a preachment of your high descent?   72
Where are your mess of sons to back you now?
The wanton Edward, and the lusty George?
And where's that valiant crook-back prodigy,
Dicky your boy, that with his grumbling voice   76
Was wont to cheer his dad in mutinies?
Or, with the rest, where is your darling Rutland?
Look, York: I stain'd this napkin with the blood
That valiant Clifford with his rapier's point   80
Made issue from the bosom of the boy;
And if thine eyes can water for his death,
I give thee this to dry thy cheeks withal.
Alas, poor York! but that I hate thee deadly,   84
I should lament thy miserable state.
I prithee grieve, to make me merry, York.
What! hath thy fiery heart so parch'd thine entrails
That not a tear can fall for Rutland's death?   88
Why art thou patient, man? thou shouldst be mad;
And I, to make thee mad, do mock thee thus.
Stamp, rave, and fret, that I may sing and dance.
Thou wouldst be fee'd, I see, to make me sport: 92
York cannot speak unless he wear a crown.
A crown for York! and, lords, bow low to him:
Hold you his hands whilst I do set it on.

           [Putting a paper crown on his head.]

Ay, marry, sir, now looks he like a king!   96
Ay, this is he that took King Henry's chair;
And this is he was his adopted heir.
But how is it that great Plantagenet

---

68 raught: *reached*   73 mess: *squad of four*
77 cheer: *incite*   83 withal: *with*   92 fee'd: *paid*

Is crown'd so soon, and broke his solemn oath?   100
As I bethink me, you should not be king
Till our King Henry had shook hands with death.
And will you pale your head in Henry's glory,
And rob his temples of the diadem,   104
Now in his life, against your holy oath?
O! 'tis a fault too-too unpardonable.
Off with the crown; and, with the crown, his head;
And, whilst we breathe, take time to do him dead.   108

    Clif. That is my office, for my father's sake.

    Queen. Nay, stay; let's hear the orisons he makes.

    York. She-wolf of France, but worse than wolves of
      France,
Whose tongue more poisons than the adder's tooth!   112
How ill-beseeming is it in thy sex
To triumph, like an Amazonian trull,
Upon their woes whom fortune captivates!
But that thy face is, vizard-like, unchanging,   116
Made impudent with use of evil deeds,
I would assay, proud queen, to make thee blush:
To tell thee whence thou cam'st, of whom deriv'd,
Were shame enough to shame thee, wert thou not
    shameless.   120
Thy father bears the type of King of Naples,
Of both the Sicils and Jerusalem;
Yet not so wealthy as an English yeoman.
Hath that poor monarch taught thee to insult?   124
It needs not, nor it boots thee not, proud queen,
Unless the adage must be verified,
That beggars mounted run their horse to death.

102 shook hands: *met*   103 pale: *encircle*
106 too-too: *altogether too*
108 breathe: *repose*   do . . . dead: *kill him*
110 orisons: *prayers*   114 trull: *virago*
115 captivates: *makes captive*   116 vizard-like: *like a mask*
117 use: *habit*   118 assay: *attempt*   121 type: *title*
125 boots: *profits*

'Tis beauty that doth oft make women proud;   128
But, God he knows, thy share thereof is small:
'Tis virtue that doth make them most admir'd;
The contrary doth make thee wonder'd at:
'Tis government that makes them seem divine;   132
The want thereof makes thee abominable.
Thou art as opposite to every good
As the Antipodes are unto us,
Or as the south to the septentrion.   136
O tiger's heart wrapp'd in a woman's hide!
How couldst thou drain the life-blood of the child,
To bid the father wipe his eyes withal,
And yet be seen to bear a woman's face?   140
Women are soft, mild, pitiful, and flexible;
Thou stern, obdurate, flinty, rough, remorseless.
Bidd'st thou me rage? why, now thou hast thy wish:
Wouldst have me weep? why, now thou hast thy
       will;   144
For raging wind blows up incessant showers,
And when the rage allays, the rain begins.
These tears are my sweet Rutland's obsequies,
And every drop cries vengeance for his death,   148
'Gainst thee, fell Clifford, and thee, false French-
       woman.
   North. Beshrew me, but his passions moves me so
That hardly can I check my eyes from tears.
   York. That face of his the hungry cannibals   152
Would not have touch'd, would not have stain'd with
       blood;
But you are more inhuman, more inexorable,—
O! ten times more, than tigers of Hyrcania.
See, ruthless queen, a hapless father's tears: 156

132 government: *conduct*   136 septentrion: *north*
137 *Cf. n.*   146 allays: *abates*   149 fell: *vindictive*
150 Beshrew: *plague on*   passions: *wild griefs*
155 Hyrcania; *cf. n.*

This cloth thou dipp'dst in blood of my sweet boy,
And I with tears do wash the blood away.
Keep thou the napkin, and go boast of this;
And if thou tell'st the heavy story right,   160
Upon my soul, the hearers will shed tears;
Yea, even my foes will shed fast-falling tears,
And say, 'Alas! it was a piteous deed!'
There, take the crown, and with the crown my
    curse,   164
And in thy need such comfort come to thee
As now I reap at thy too cruel hand!
Hard-hearted Clifford, take me from the world;
My soul to heaven, my blood upon your heads!   168
    North. Had he been slaughter-man to all my kin,
I should not for my life but weep with him,
To see how inly sorrow gripes his soul.
    Queen. What! weeping-ripe, my Lord Northumber-
    land?   172
Think but upon the wrong he did us all,
And that will quickly dry thy melting tears.
    Clif. Here's for my oath; here's for my father's
    death.   [*Stabbing him.*]
    Queen. And here's to right our gentle-hearted king.
                              [*Stabbing him.*]
    York. Open thy gate of mercy, gracious God!
My soul flies through these wounds to seek out thee.
                                   [*Dies.*]
    Queen. Off with his head, and set it on York gates;
So York may overlook the town of York.   180
                            Flourish. Exeunt.

159 napkin: *handkerchief*   160 heavy: *grievous*
164 *Cf. n.*   171 inly: *inward*
172 weeping-ripe: *ready for tears*

Is kindling coals that fires all my breast,
And burns me up with flames, that tears would
　　quench.　　84
To weep is to make less the depth of grief:
Tears then, for babes; blows and revenge for me!
Richard, I bear thy name; I'll venge thy death,
Or die renowned by attempting it.　　88

　　Edw. His name that valiant duke hath left with thee;
His dukedom and his chair with me is left.

　　Rich. Nay, if thou be that princely eagle's bird,
Show thy descent by gazing 'gainst the sun:　　92
For chair and dukedom, throne and kingdom say;
Either that is thine, or else thou wert not his.

*March.　Enter Warwick, Marquess Montague, and
　　　　their Army.*

　　War. How now, fair lords! What fare? what news
　　abroad?

　　Rich. Great Lord of Warwick, if we should re-
　　count　　9
Our baleful news, and at each word's deliverance
Stab poniards in our flesh till all were told,
The words would add more anguish than the wounds.
O valiant lord! the Duke of York is slain.　　10

　　Edw. O Warwick! Warwick! that Plantagenet
Which held thee dearly as his soul's redemption,
Is by the stern Lord Clifford done to death.

　　War. Ten days ago I drown'd these news i
　　tears,　　1
And now, to add more measure to your woes,
I come to tell you things sith then befallen.
After the bloody fray at Wakefield fought,
Where your brave father breath'd his latest gasp,　　1

90 chair: *seat of authority*　　　　　91, 92 *Cf.*
91 bird: *fledgling*　　　　95 What fare: *how do you fa*

ACT SECOND

Scene One

[Chipping Norton in Oxfordshire]

A March.　Enter Edward, Richard, and their power.

　　Edw. I wonder how our princely father 'scap'd,
Or whether he be 'scap'd away or no
From Clifford's and Northumberland's pursuit.
Had he been ta'en, we should have heard the news;　　4
Had he been slain, we should have heard the news;
Or had he 'scap'd, methinks we should have heard
The happy tidings of his good escape.
How fares my brother? why is he so sad?　　8

　　Rich. I cannot joy until I be resolv'd
Where our right valiant father is become.
I saw him in the battle range about,
And watch'd him how he singled Clifford forth.　　12
Methought he bore him in the thickest troop
As doth a lion in a herd of neat;
Or as a bear, encompass'd round with dogs,
Who having pinch'd a few and made them cry,　　16
The rest stand all aloof and bark at him.
So far'd our father with his enemies;
So fled his enemies my warlike father:
Methinks 'tis prize enough to be his son.　　20
See how the morning opes her golden gates,
And takes her farewell of the glorious sun;
How well resembles it the prime of youth,
Trimm'd like a younker prancing to his love.　　24

9 resolv'd: *informed*
10 Where . . . is become: *what has become of*
13 bore him: *behaved himself*
14 neat: *cattle*　　　　　　　　20 prize; *cf. n.*
22 *Takes leaves of the sun as it sets out on its daily course*
23 prime: *springtime*　　　　24 younker: *stripling*

Edw. Dazzle mine eyes, or do I see three suns?

Rich. Three glorious suns, each one a perfect sun;
Not separated with the racking clouds,
But sever'd in a pale clear-shining sky.   28
See, see! they join, embrace, and seem to kiss,
As if they vow'd some league inviolable:
Now are they but one lamp, one light, one sun.
In this the heaven figures some event.   32

    Edw. 'Tis wondrous strange, the like yet never
    heard of.
I think it cites us, brother, to the field;
That we, the sons of brave Plantagenet,
Each one already blazing by our meeds,   36
Should notwithstanding join our lights together,
And over-shine the earth, as this the world.
Whate'er it bodes, henceforward will I bear
Upon my target three fair-shining suns.   40

    Rich. Nay, bear three daughters: by your leave I
    speak it,
You love the breeder better than the male.

Enter one blowing.

But what art thou, whose heavy looks foretell
Some dreadful story hanging on thy tongue?   44

    Mess. Ah! one that was a woeful looker-on,
When as the noble Duke of York was slain,
Your princely father, and my loving lord.

    Edw. O! speak no more, for I have heard too
    much.   48

    Rich. Say how he died, for I will hear it all.

    Mess. Environed he was with many foes,

And stood against them, as the hope of Troy
Against the Greeks that would have enter'd Tr[oy]
But Hercules himself must yield to odds;
And many strokes, though with a little axe,
Hews down and fells the hardest-timber'd oak.
By many hands your father was subdu'd;
But only slaughter'd by the ireful arm
Of unrelenting Clifford and the queen,
Who crown'd the gracious duke in high despite[,]
Laugh'd in his face; and when with grief he we[pt]
The ruthless queen gave him to dry his cheeks
A napkin steeped in the harmless blood
Of sweet young Rutland, by rough Clifford slai[n]
And after many scorns, many foul taunts,
They took his head, and on the gates of York
They set the same; and there it doth remain,
The saddest spectacle that e'er I view'd.

    Edw. Sweet Duke of York! our prop to lean u[pon]
Now thou art gone, we have no staff, no stay!
O Clifford! boist'rous Clifford! thou hast slain
The flower of Europe for his chivalry;
And treacherously hast thou vanquish'd him,
For hand to hand he would have vanquish'd the[e]
Now my soul's palace is become a prison:
Ah! would she break from hence, that this my [body]
Might in the ground be closed up in rest,
For never henceforth shall I joy again,
Never, O! never, shall I see more joy.

    Rich. I cannot weep, for all my body's mois[ture]
Scarce serves to quench my furnace-burning he[art]
Nor can my tongue unload my heart's great bur[den]
For self-same wind that I should speak withal

---

25 *Cf. n.*
27 racking: *driving in soft masses*
32 figures: *foreshadows*   event: *future happening*
34 cites: *calls*   36 meeds: *merits*
38 this: *this light, the sun*
41 by your leave: *without meaning offense*

51 the hope of Troy: *Hector*   68
71 *Him who in knightly prowess was the pride of Europe*
80 furnace-burning: *burning like a furnace*

Tidings, as swiftly as the posts could run,
Were brought me of your loss and his depart.
I, then in London, keeper of the king,
Muster'd my soldiers, gather'd flocks of friends,   112
[And very well appointed, as I thought,]
March'd towards Saint Albans to intercept the queen,
Bearing the king in my behalf along;
For by my scouts I was advertised   116
That she was coming with a full intent
To dash our late decree in parliament,
Touching King Henry's oath and your succession.
Short tale to make, we at Saint Albans met,   120
Our battles join'd, and both sides fiercely fought:
But whether 'twas the coldness of the king,
Who look'd full gently on his warlike queen,
That robb'd my soldiers of their heated spleen;   124
Or whether 'twas report of her success;
Or more than common fear of Clifford's rigour,
Who thunders to his captives blood and death,
I cannot judge: but, to conclude with truth,   128
Their weapons like to lightning came and went;
Our soldiers', like the night-owl's lazy flight,
Or like a lazy thresher with a flail,
Fell gently down, as if they struck their friends.   132
I cheer'd them up with justice of our cause,
With promise of high pay, and great rewards:
But all in vain; they had no heart to fight,
And we in them no hope to win the day;   136
So that we fled: the king unto the queen;
Lord George your brother, Norfolk, and myself,
In haste, post-haste, are come to join with you;

110 depart: *decease*   113 appointed: *equipped; cf. n.*
116 advertised: *informed*   118 dash: *frustrate*
124 heated spleen: *hot valor*   138 Lord George: *Clarence*
139 haste, post-haste: *the greatest possible speed*

For in the marches here we heard you were,   140
Making another head to fight again.

   Edw. Where is the Duke of Norfolk, gentle War-
     wick?
And when came George from Burgundy to England?

   War. Some six miles off the duke is with the sol-
     diers;   144
And for your brother, he was lately sent
From your kind aunt, Duchess of Burgundy,
With aid of soldiers to this needful war.

   Rich. 'Twas odds, belike, when valiant Warwick
     fled: 148
Oft have I heard his praises in pursuit,
But ne'er till now his scandal of retire.

   War. Nor now my scandal, Richard, dost thou hear;
For thou shalt know, this strong right hand of mine 152
Can pluck the diadem from faint Henry's head,
And wring the awful sceptre from his fist,
Were he as famous, and as bold in war
As he is fam'd for mildness, peace, and prayer.   156

   Rich. I know it well, Lord Warwick; blame me not:
'Tis love I bear thy glories makes me speak.
But in this troublous time what's to be done?
Shall we go throw away our coats of steel,   160
And wrap our bodies in black mourning gowns,
Numb'ring our Ave-Maries with our beads?
Or shall we on the helmets of our foes
Tell our devotion with revengeful arms?   164
If for the last, say 'Ay,' and to it, lords.

   War. Why, therefore Warwick came to seek you out;
And therefore comes my brother Montague.

---

140 marches: *borders (of Wales)*   141 head: *armed force*
146 Duchess of Burgundy; *cf. n.*
148 'Twas odds, belike: *the odds must have been great*
150 scandal of retire: *disgrace through retreat*
164 Tell . . . devotion: *say our prayers, show our love (pun)*

Attend me, lords.   The proud insulting queen,   168
With Clifford and the haught Northumberland,
And of their feather many moe proud birds,
Have wrought the easy-melting king like wax.
He swore consent to your succession,   172
His oath enrolled in the parliament;
And now to London all the crew are gone,
To frustrate both his oath and what beside
May make against the house of Lancaster.   176
Their power, I think, is thirty thousand strong:
Now, if the help of Norfolk and myself,
With all the friends that thou, brave Earl of March,
Amongst the loving Welshmen canst procure,   180
Will but amount to five and twenty thousand,
Why, *Via!* to London will we march,
And once again bestride our foaming steeds,
And once again cry, 'Charge upon our foes!'   184
But never once again turn back and fly.

    Rich. Ay, now methinks I hear great Warwick
      speak:
Ne'er may he live to see a sunshine day,
That cries 'Retire,' if Warwick bid him stay.   188

    Edw. Lord Warwick, on thy shoulder will I lean;
And when thou fail'st—as God forbid the hour!—
Must Edward fall, which peril heaven forfend!

    War. No longer Earl of March, but Duke of
      York: 192
The next degree is England's royal throne;
For King of England shalt thou be proclaim'd
In every borough as we pass along;
And he that throws not up his cap for joy   196
Shall for the fault make forfeit of his head.

169 haught: *proud*   170 moe: *more*
171 wrought: *worked, moulded*
173 enrolled: *formally written in a parchment roll*
182 Via: *forward*   187 sunshine: *bright*   193 degree: *step*

King Edward, valiant Richard, Montague,
Stay we no longer dreaming of renown,
But sound the trumpets, and about our task.   200
   Rich. Then, Clifford, were thy heart as hard as
     steel,—
As thou hast shown it flinty by thy deeds,—
I come to pierce it, or to give thee mine.
   Edw. Then strike up, drums! God, and Saint
     George for us!   204

Enter a Messenger.

   War. How now! what news?
   Mess. The Duke of Norfolk sends you word by me,
The queen is coming with a puissant host;
And craves your company for speedy counsel.   208
   War. Why then it sorts; brave warriors, let's away.
                        Exeunt omnes.

Scene Two

[*Before York*]

*Flourish.   Enter the King, the Queen, Clifford,
   Northumberland, and young Prince, with drum and
   trumpets.*

   Queen. Welcome, my lord, to this brave town of
     York.
Yonder's the head of that arch-enemy,
That sought to be encompass'd with your crown:
Doth not the object cheer your heart, my lord?   4
   King. Ay, as the rocks cheer them that fear their
     wrack:
To see this sight, it irks my very soul.

209 sorts: *turns out well*

Withhold revenge, dear God! 'tis not my fault,
Nor wittingly have I infring'd my vow.   8
   Clif. My gracious liege, this too much lenity
And harmful pity must be laid aside.
To whom do lions cast their gentle looks?
Not to the beast that would usurp their den.   12
Whose hand is that the forest bear doth lick?
Not his that spoils her young before her face.
Who 'scapes the lurking serpent's mortal sting?
Not he that sets his foot upon her back.   16
The smallest worm will turn being trodden on,
And doves will peck in safeguard of their brood.
Ambitious York did level at thy crown,
Thou smiling while he knit his angry brows: 20
He, but a duke, would have his son a king,
And raise his issue like a loving sire;
Thou, being a king, bless'd with a goodly son,
Didst yield consent to disinherit him,   24
Which argu'd thee a most unloving father.
Unreasonable creatures feed their young;
And though man's face be fearful to their eyes,
Yet, in protection of their tender ones,   28
Who hath not seen them, even with those wings
Which sometime they have us'd with fearful flight,
Make war with him that climb'd unto their nest,
Offering their own lives in their young's defence?   32
For shame, my liege! make them your precedent.
Were it not pity that this goodly boy
Should lose his birthright by his father's fault,
And long hereafter say unto his child,   36
'What my great grandfather and grandsire got,
My careless father fondly gave away?'
Ah! what a shame were this.   Look on the boy;

18 safeguard: *protection*   19 level: *aim*   22 raise: *ennoble*
33 precedent: *example*   38 fondly: *foolishly*

And let his manly face, which promiseth   40
Successful fortune, steel thy melting heart
To hold thine own and leave thine own with him.

   King. Full well hath Clifford play'd the orator,
Inferring arguments of mighty force.   44
But, Clifford, tell me, didst thou never hear
That things ill got had ever bad success?
And happy always was it for that son
Whose father for his hoarding went to hell?   48
I'll leave my son my virtuous deeds behind;
And would my father had left me no more!
For all the rest is held at such a rate
As brings a thousand-fold more care to keep   52
Than in possession any jot of pleasure.
Ah! cousin York, would thy best friends did know
How it doth grieve me that thy head is here!

   Queen. My lord, cheer up your spirits: our foes are
      nigh,   56
And this soft courage makes your followers faint.
You promis'd knighthood to our forward son:
Unsheathe your sword, and dub him presently.
Edward, kneel down.   60

   King. Edward Plantagenet, arise a knight;
And learn this lesson, draw thy sword in right.

   Prince. My gracious father, by your kingly leave,
I'll draw it as apparent to the crown,   64
And in that quarrel use it to the death.

   Clif. Why, that is spoken like a toward prince.

Enter a Messenger.

   Mess. Royal commanders, be in readiness:
For with a band of thirty thousand men   68

44 Inferring: *alleging*
47 happy . . . it: *did things always turn out well*
58 forward: *ardent*
64 apparent: *heir-apparent*   66 toward: *hopeful*

Comes Warwick, backing of the Duke of York;
And in the towns, as they do march along,
Proclaims him king, and many fly to him:
Darraign your battle, for they are at hand.   72

Clif. I would your highness would depart the field:
The queen hath best success when you are absent.

   Queen. Ay, good my lord, and leave us to our fortune.

   King. Why, that's my fortune too; therefore I'll stay.   76

   North. Be it with resolution then to fight.

   Prince. My royal father, cheer these noble lords,
And hearten those that fight in your defence:
Unsheathe your sword, good father: cry, 'Saint George!'   80

*March. Enter Edward, Warwick, Richard, Clarence,
      Norfolk, Montague, and Soldiers.*

   Edw. Now, perjur'd Henry, wilt thou kneel for grace,
And set thy diadem upon my head;
Or bide the mortal fortune of the field?

   Queen. Go, rate thy minions, proud insulting boy! 84
Becomes it thee to be thus bold in terms
Before thy sovereign and thy lawful king?

   Edw. I am his king, and he should bow his knee;
I was adopted heir by his consent: 88
Since when, his oath is broke; for, as I hear,
You, that are king, though he do wear the crown,
Have caus'd him, by new act of parliament,
To blot out me, and put his own son in.   92

   Clif. And reason too:

---

72 Darraign: *draw up*   battle: *line of battle*   73 depart: *leave*
76 *Cf. n.*   84 rate: *scold*   minions: *saucy favorites*
85 thus . . . terms: *on so insolent a footing*   89-92 *Cf. n.*
93 reason: *it was reasonable*

Who should succeed the father but the son?

    Rich. Are you there, butcher? O! I cannot speak.

    Clif. Ay, crook-back; here I stand to answer thee, 96
Or any he the proudest of thy sort.

    Rich. 'Twas you that kill'd young Rutland, was it
      not?

    Clif. Ay, and old York, and yet not satisfied.

    Rich. For God's sake, lords, give signal to the
      fight.   100

    War. What sayst thou, Henry, wilt thou yield the
      crown?

    Queen. Why, how now, long-tongu'd Warwick! dare
      you speak?
When you and I met at Saint Albans last,
Your legs did better service than your hands.   104

    War. Then 'twas my turn to fly, and now 'tis thine.

    Clif. You said so much before, and yet you fled.

    War. 'Twas not your valour, Clifford, drove me
      thence.

    North. No, nor your manhood that durst make you
      stay.   108

    Rich. Northumberland, I hold thee reverently.
Break off the parley; for scarce I can refrain
The execution of my big-swoln heart
Upon that Clifford, that cruel child-killer.   112

    Clif. I slew thy father: call'st thou him a child?

    Rich. Ay, like a dastard and a treacherous coward,
As thou didst kill our tender brother Rutland;
But ere sunset I'll make thee curse the deed.   116

    King. Have done with words, my lords, and hear me
      speak.

    Queen. Defy them, then, or else hold close thy lips.

97 any . . . proudest: *the proudest one whatever*   sort: *party*
109 reverently: *in respect*

King. I prithee, give no limits to my tongue:
I am a king, and privileg'd to speak.   120
    Clif. My liege, the wound that bred this meeting here
Cannot be cur'd by words; therefore be still.
    Rich. Then, executioner, unsheathe thy sword.
By him that made us all, I am resolv'd   124
That Clifford's manhood lies upon his tongue.
    Edw. Say, Henry, shall I have my right or no?
A thousand men have broke their fasts to-day,
That ne'er shall dine unless thou yield the crown.   128
    War. If thou deny, their blood upon thy head;
For York in justice puts his armour on.
    Prince. If that be right which Warwick says is right,
There is no wrong, but everything is right.   132
    Rich. Whoever got thee, there thy mother stands;
For well I wot thou hast thy mother's tongue.
    Queen. But thou art neither like thy sire nor dam,
But like a foul misshapen stigmatic,   136
Mark'd by the destinies to be avoided,
As venom toads, or lizards' dreadful stings.
    Rich. Iron of Naples hid with English gilt,—
Whose father bears the title of a king,   140
As if a channel should be call'd the sea,—
Sham'st thou not, knowing whence thou art extraught,
To let thy tongue detect thy base-born heart?
    Edw. A wisp of straw were worth a thousand crowns,   144
To make this shameless callet know herself.

119 limits: *limitation*   124 resolv'd: *convinced*
129 deny: *refuse*   130 in . . . on: *fights in a just cause*
133 got: *begot*   136 stigmatic: *one branded by deformity*
138 venom: *poisonous*
139 *You whose cheap Neapolitan origin is gilded by your English rank*
141 channel: *gutter*   142 extraught: *extracted*
144 wisp of straw; *cf. n.*   145 callet: *lewd woman*

Helen of Greece was fairer far than thou,
Although thy husband may be Menelaus;
And ne'er was Agamemnon's brother wrong'd   148
By that false woman as this king by thee.
His father revell'd in the heart of France,
And tam'd the king, and made the Dauphin stoop;
And had he match'd according to his state,   152
He might have kept that glory to this day;
But when he took a beggar to his bed,
And grac'd thy poor sire with his bridal day,
Even then that sunshine brew'd a shower for him,   156
That wash'd his father's fortunes forth of France,
And heap'd sedition on his crown at home.
For what hath broach'd this tumult but thy pride?
Hadst thou been meek our title still had slept,   160
And we, in pity of the gentle king,
Had slipp'd our claim until another age.
        Clar. But when we saw our sunshine made thy
            spring,
And that thy summer bred us no increase,   164
We set the axe to thy usurping root;
And though the edge hath something hit ourselves,
Yet know thou, since we have begun to strike,
We'll never leave, till we have hewn thee down,   168
Or bath'd thy growing with our heated bloods.
        Edw. And in this resolution I defy thee;
Not willing any longer conference,
Since thou deny'st the gentle king to speak.   172
Sound trumpets!—let our bloody colours wave!
And either victory, or else a grave.
        Queen. Stay, Edward.

147 Menelaus: *the typical injured husband*   155 *Cf. n.*
162 slipp'd: *let pass, forgone*   164 increase: *harvest*
166 something: *somewhat*
169 bath'd thy growing: *watered thy roots*   172 deny'st: *forbiddest*

Edw. No, wrangling woman, we'll no longer stay:
These words will cost ten thousand lives this day.

　　　　　　　　　　　　　　　　Exeunt omnes.

Scene Three

[*A Field of Battle between Towton and Saxton, in
Yorkshire*]

　　Alarum. Excursions. Enter Warwick.

War. Forspent with toil, as runners with a race,
I lay me down a little while to breathe;
For strokes receiv'd, and many blows repaid,
Have robb'd my strong-knit sinews of their strength, 4
And spite of spite needs must I rest a while.

　　　　　Enter Edward, running.

Edw. Smile, gentle heaven! or strike, ungentle
　　death!
For this world frowns, and Edward's sun is clouded.
　War. How now, my lord! what hap? what hope of
　　good?　　　　　　　　　　　　　　　　8

　　　　　　Enter Clarence.

Clar. Our hap is loss, our hope but sad despair,
Our ranks are broke, and ruin follows us.
What counsel give you? whither shall we fly?　　11
　Edw. Bootless is flight, they follow us with wings;
And weak we are and cannot shun pursuit.

　　　　　　Enter Richard.

Rich. Ah! Warwick, why hast thou withdrawn thy-
　　self?
Thy brother's blood the thirsty earth hath drunk,

1 Forspent: *utterly exhausted; cf. n.*　　　8 hap: *fortune*
12 Bootless: *fruitless*　　　15 Thy brother's blood; *cf. n.*

Broach'd with the steely point of Clifford's lance;   16
And in the very pangs of death he cried,
Like to a dismal clangor heard from far,
'Warwick, revenge! brother, revenge my death!'
So, underneath the belly of their steeds,   20
That stain'd their fetlocks in his smoking blood,
The noble gentleman gave up the ghost.

War. Then let the earth be drunken with our blood:
I'll kill my horse because I will not fly.   24
Why stand we like soft-hearted women here,
Wailing our losses, whiles the foe doth rage;
And look upon, as if the tragedy
Were play'd in jest by counterfeiting actors?   28
Here on my knee I vow to God above,
I'll never pause again, never stand still,
Till either death hath clos'd these eyes of mine,
Or fortune given me measure of revenge.   32

Edw. O Warwick! I do bend my knee with thine;
And in this vow do chain my soul to thine.
And, ere my knee rise from the earth's cold face,
I throw my hands, mine eyes, my heart to thee,   36
Thou setter up and plucker down of kings,
Beseeching thee, if with thy will it stands
That to my foes this body must be prey,
Yet that thy brazen gates of heaven may ope,   40
And give sweet passage to my sinful soul!
Now, lords, take leave until we meet again,
Where'er it be, in heaven or in earth.

Rich. Brother, give me thy hand; and, gentle War-
            wick,   44
Let me embrace thee in my weary arms:
I, that did never weep, now melt with woe
That winter should cut off our spring-time so.

16 Broach'd: *set flowing*   27 upon: *on*
32 measure: *due proportion*   38 stands: *accords*

War. Away, away! Once more, sweet lords, farewell.   48

 Clar. Yet let us all together to our troops,
And give them leave to fly that will not stay,
And call them pillars that will stand to us;
And if we thrive, promise them such rewards 52
As victors wear at the Olympian games.
This may plant courage in their quailing breasts;
For yet is hope of life and victory.
Forslow no longer; make we hence amain. 56

             Exeunt.

Scene Four

[*Another Part of the Field*]

Excursions. Enter Richard and Clifford.

 Rich. Now, Clifford, I have singled thee alone.
Suppose this arm is for the Duke of York,
And this for Rutland; both bound to revenge,
Wert thou environ'd with a brazen wall. 4

 Clif. Now, Richard, I am with thee here alone.
This is the hand that stabb'd thy father York,
And this the hand that slew thy brother Rutland;
And here's the heart that triumphs in their death 8
And cheers these hands that slew thy sire and brother,
To execute the like upon thyself;
And so, have at thee!

     They fight. Warwick comes. Clifford flies.

 Rich. Nay, Warwick, single out some other chase; 12
For I myself will hunt this wolf to death.

             Exeunt.

---

56 Forslow: *delay*
1 singled: *selected one victim from the herd (hunting term)*
9 cheers: *encourages*

Scene Five

[Another Part of the Field]

Alarum.   Enter King Henry alone.

Hen. This battle fares like to the morning's **war,**
When dying clouds contend with growing light,
What time the shepherd, blowing of his nails,
Can neither call it perfect day nor night.   4
Now sways it this way, like a mighty sea
Forc'd by the tide to combat with the wind;
Now sways it that way, like the self-same sea
Forc'd to retire by fury of the wind: 8
Sometime the flood prevails, and then the wind;
Now one the better, then another best;
Both tugging to be victors, breast to breast,
Yet neither conqueror nor conquered: 12
So is the equal poise of this fell war.
Here on this molehill will I sit me down.
To whom God will, there be the victory!
For Margaret my queen, and Clifford too,   16
Have chid me from the battle; swearing both
They prosper best of all when I am thence.
Would I were dead! if God's good will were so;
For what is in this world but grief and woe?   20
O God! methinks it were a happy life,
To be no better than a homely swain;
To sit upon a hill, as I do now,
To carve out dials quaintly, point by point,   24
Thereby to see the minutes how they run,
How many make the hour full complete;
How many hours bring about the day;
How many days will finish up the year;   28

3 blowing of: *warming by breathing on*
24 dials: *sundials*   quaintly: *ingeniously*

How many years a mortal man may live.
When this is known, then to divide the times:
So many hours must I tend my flock;
So many hours must I take my rest;   32
So many hours must I contemplate;
So many hours must I sport myself;
So many days my ewes have been with young;
So many weeks ere the poor fools will ean;   36
So many years ere I shall shear the fleece:
So minutes, hours, days, months, and years,
Pass'd over to the end they were created,
Would bring white hairs unto a quiet grave.   40
Ah! what a life were this! how sweet! how lovely!
Gives not the hawthorn bush a sweeter shade
To shepherds, looking on their silly sheep,
Than doth a rich embroider'd canopy   44
To kings, that fear their subjects' treachery?
O, yes! it doth; a thousand-fold it doth.
And to conclude, the shepherd's homely curds,
His cold thin drink out of his leather bottle,   48
His wonted sleep under a fresh tree's shade,
All which secure and sweetly he enjoys,
Is far beyond a prince's delicates,
His viands sparkling in a golden cup,   52
His body couched in a curious bed,
When care, mistrust, and treason wait on him.

*Alarum. Enter a Son that hath killed his Father at
one door: and a Father that hath killed his Son at
another door.*

    Son. Ill blows the wind that profits nobody.
This man whom hand to hand I slew in fight   56

34 sport: *amuse*   36 ean: *give birth*
43 silly: *harmless*   50 secure: *securely*
51 delicates: *dainties*   53 curious: *gorgeous*   54 *Cf. n.*

May be possessed with some store of crowns;
And I, that haply take them from him now,
May yet ere night yield both my life and them
To some man else, as this dead man doth me.   60
Who's this?   O God! it is my father's face,
Whom in this conflict I unwares have kill'd.
O heavy times, begetting such events!
From London by the king was I press'd forth;   64
My father, being the Earl of Warwick's man,
Came on the part of York, press'd by his master;
And I, who at his hands receiv'd my life,
Have by my hands of life bereaved him.   68
Pardon me, God, I knew not what I did!
And pardon, father, for I knew not thee!
My tears shall wipe away these bloody marks;
And no more words till they have flow'd their fill.   72
    King. O piteous spectacle!   O bloody times!
Whiles lions war and battle for their dens,
Poor harmless lambs abide their enmity.
Weep, wretched man, I'll aid thee tear for tear;   76
And let our hearts and eyes, like civil war,
Be blind with tears, and break o'ercharg'd with grief.

Enter Father, bearing of his Son.

    Fath. Thou that so stoutly hast resisted me,
Give me thy gold, if thou hast any gold,   80
For I have bought it with an hundred blows.
But let me see: is this our foeman's face?
Ah! no, no, no, it is mine only son.
Ah, boy, if any life be left in thee,   84
Throw up thine eye: see, see! what showers arise,
Blown with the windy tempest of my heart,

---

57 with: *of*   store: *quantity*   58 haply: *by chance*
62 unwares: *unknowingly*
64 press'd forth: *led out by impressment*   78 S. d.; *cf. n.*

Upon thy wounds, that kills mine eye and heart.
O! pity, God, this miserable age.   88
What stratagems, how fell, how butcherly,
Erroneous, mutinous, and unnatural,
This deadly quarrel daily doth beget!
O boy! thy father gave thee life too soon,   92
And hath bereft thee of thy life too late.
  King. Woe above woe! grief more than common
    grief!
O! that my death would stay these ruthful deeds.
O! pity, pity; gentle heaven, pity.   96
The red rose and the white are on his face,
The fatal colours of our striving houses:
The one his purple blood right well resembles;
The other his pale cheeks, methinks, presenteth: 100
Wither one rose, and let the other flourish!
If you contend, a thousand lives must wither.
  Son. How will my mother for a father's death
Take on with me and ne'er be satisfied!   104
  Fath. How will my wife for slaughter of my son
Shed seas of tears and ne'er be satisfied!
  King. How will the country for these woeful chances
Misthink the king and not be satisfied!   108
  Son. Was ever son so ru'd a father's death?
  Fath. Was ever father so bemoan'd his son?
  King. Was ever king so griev'd for subjects' woe?
Much is your sorrow; mine, ten times so much.   112
  Son. I'll bear thee hence, where I may weep my fill.
          [*Exit with the body.*]
  Fath. These arms of mine shall be thy winding-
    sheet;

87 Upon: *at sight of*   90 Erroneous: *criminal*
93 late: *recently*   95 ruthful: *pitiable*
100 presenteth: *symbolize*   104 Take on: *rave*
108 Misthink: *think ill of*

My heart, sweet boy, shall be thy sepulchre,
For from my heart thine image ne'er shall go: 116
My sighing breast shall be thy funeral bell;
And so obsequious will thy father be,
E'en for the loss of thee, having no more,
As Priam was for all his valiant sons.   120
I'll bear thee hence; and let them fight that will,
For I have murther'd where I should not kill.

Exit [*with the body*].

Hen. Sad-hearted men, much overgone with care,
Here sits a king more woeful than you are.   124

*Alarums. Excursions. Enter the Queen, the Prince,
and Exeter.*

Prince. Fly, father, fly! for all your friends are fled,
And Warwick rages like a chafed bull.
Away! for death doth hold us in pursuit.

Queen. Mount you, my lord; towards Berwick post
    amain.   128
Edward and Richard, like a brace of greyhounds
Having the fearful flying hare in sight,
With fiery eyes sparkling for very wrath,
And bloody steel grasp'd in their ireful hands,   132
Are at our backs; and therefore hence amain.

Exe. Away! for vengeance comes along with them.
Nay, stay not to expostulate; make speed,
Or else come after: I'll away before.   136

Hen. Nay, take me with thee, good sweet Exeter:
Not that I fear to stay, but love to go
Whither the queen intends.   Forward! away!

Exeunt.

118 obsequious: *dutiful in mourning*   123 overgone: *oppressed*
126 chafed: *angered*   131 very: *veritable*

Scene Six

[*The Same*]

A loud alarum.   Enter Clifford, wounded.

Clif. Here burns my candle out; ay, here it dies,
Which, whiles it lasted, gave King Henry light.
O Lancaster! I fear thy overthrow
More than my body's parting with my soul.   4
My love and fear glu'd many friends to thee;
And, now I fall, thy tough commixtures melts,
Impairing Henry, strength'ning misproud York:
[The common people swarm like summer flies;]   8
And whither fly the gnats but to the sun?
And who shines now but Henry's enemies?
O Phœbus! hadst thou never given consent
That Phaethon should check thy fiery steeds,   12
Thy burning car never had scorch'd the earth;
And, Henry, hadst thou sway'd as kings should do,
Or as thy father and his father did,
Giving no ground unto the house of York,   16
They never then had sprung like summer flies;
I and ten thousand in this luckless realm
Had left no mourning widows for our death,
And thou this day hadst kept thy chair in peace.   20
For what doth cherish weeds but gentle air?
And what makes robbers bold but too much lenity?
Bootless are plaints, and cureless are my wounds;
No way to fly, nor strength to hold out flight: 24
The foe is merciless, and will not pity,
For at their hands I have deserv'd no pity.
The air hath got into my deadly wounds,

Scene Six S. d.; *cf. n.*   5 My . . . fear: *love and fear of me*
6 commixtures: *compounds, substances held together by glue*
7 Impairing: *weakening*   8 *Cf. n.*
12 check: *curb, manage*   17 sprung: *propagated*

And much effuse of blood doth make me faint.   28
Come, York and Richard, Warwick and the rest;
I stabb'd your fathers' bosoms, split my breast.
                                        [*He faints.*]

Alarum and Retreat.   Enter Edward, Warwick, Rich-
ard, and Soldiers, Montague and Clarence.

   Edw. Now breathe we, lords: good fortune bids us
     pause,
And smooth the frowns of war with peaceful looks. 32
Some troops pursue the bloody-minded queen,
That led calm Henry, though he were a king,
As doth a sail, fill'd with a fretting gust,
Command an argosy to stem the waves.   36
But think you, lords, that Clifford fled with them?
   War. No, 'tis impossible he should escape;
For, though before his face I speak the words,
Your brother Richard mark'd him for the grave;   40
And wheresoe'er he is, he's surely dead.
                 Clifford groans [*and dies*].
   Edw. Whose soul is that which takes her heavy
     leave?
   Rich. A deadly groan, like life and death's de-
     parting.
   Edw. See who it is: and now the battle's ended,   44
If friend or foe let him be gently us'd.
   Rich. Revoke that doom of mercy, for 'tis Clifford;
Who not contented that he lopp'd the branch
In hewing Rutland when his leaves put forth,   48
But set his murth'ring knife unto the root
From whence that tender spray did sweetly spring,
I mean our princely father, Duke of York.

28 effuse: *shedding.*
42-44 *Cf. n.*
48 when . . . forth: *in youth*

36 argosy: *large merchant vessel*
           46 doom: *judgment*
           49 But set; *cf. n.*

War. From off the gates of York fetch down the
　head,　　　52
Your father's head, which Clifford placed there;
Instead whereof let this supply the room:
Measure for measure must be answered.

Edw. Bring forth that fatal screech-owl to our
　house,　　　56
That nothing sung but death to us and ours:
Now death shall stop his dismal threatening sound,
And his ill-boding tongue no more shall speak.

War. I think his understanding is bereft.　　　60
Speak, Clifford; dost thou know who speaks to thee?
Dark cloudy death o'ershades his beams of life,
And he nor sees, nor hears us what we say.

Rich. O! would he did; and so perhaps he doth·　64
'Tis but his policy to counterfeit,
Because he would avoid such bitter taunts
Which in the time of death he gave our father.

Clar. If so thou think'st, vex him with eager
　words.　　　68

Rich. Clifford! ask mercy and obtain no grace.

Edw. Clifford, repent in bootless penitence.

War. Clifford! devise excuses for thy faults.

Clar. While we devise fell tortures for thy faults.　72

Rich. Thou didst love York, and I am son to York.

Edw. Thou pitiedst Rutland, I will pity thee.

Clar. Where's Captain Margaret, to fence you now?

War. They mock thee, Clifford: swear as thou wast
　wont.　　　76

Rich. What! not an oath? nay, then the world goes
　hard

---

54 supply the room: *take its place*
55 *Treatment given must correspond to treatment received*
60 understanding: *consciousness*　　　67 Which: *as*
68 eager: *biting*　　　75 fence: *shield*
77 goes hard: *has come to a hard pass*

When Clifford cannot spare his friends an oath.
I know by that he's dead; and, by my soul,
If this right hand would buy two hours' life, 80
That I in all despite might rail at him,
This hand should chop it off, and with the issuing
    blood
Stifle the villain whose unstaunched thirst
York and young Rutland could not satisfy. 84

   War. Ay, but he's dead: off with the traitor's head,
And rear it in the place your father's stands.
And now to London with triumphant march,
There to be crowned England's royal king: 88
From whence shall Warwick cut the sea to France,
And ask the Lady Bona for thy queen.
So shalt thou sinew both these lands together;
And, having France thy friend, thou shalt not dread 92
The scatter'd foe that hopes to rise again;
For though they cannot greatly sting to hurt,
Yet look to have them buzz to offend thine ears.
First will I see the coronation; 96
And then to Brittany I'll cross the sea,
To effect this marriage, so it please my lord.

   Edw. Even as thou wilt, sweet Warwick, let it be;
For in thy shoulder do I build my seat, 100
And never will I undertake the thing
Wherein thy counsel and consent is wanting.
Richard, I will create thee Duke of Gloucester;
And George, of Clarence; Warwick, as ourself, 104
Shall do and undo as him pleaseth best.

   Rich. Let me be Duke of Clarence, George of
    Gloucester,
For Gloucester's dukedom is too ominous.

   War. Tut! that's a foolish observation: 108

---

81 despite: *obloquy*   83 unstaunched: *insatiable*
90 Lady Bona; *cf. n.*   91 sinew: *join*   107 *Cf. n.*

Richard, be Duke of Gloucester.   Now to London,
To see these honours in possession.   *Exeunt.*

ACT THIRD

Scene One

[A Chase in the North of England]

*Enter Sinklo and Humphrey [two gamekeepers], with
cross-bows in their hands.*

Sink. Under this thick-grown brake we'll shroud
    ourselves;
For through this laund anon the deer will come;
And in this covert will we make our stand,
Culling the principal of all the deer.   4
    Hum. I'll stay above the hill, so both may shoot.
    Sink. That cannot be; the noise of thy cross-bow
Will scare the herd, and so my shoot is lost.
Here stand we both, and aim we at the best: 8
And, for the time shall not seem tedious,
I'll tell thee what befell me on a day
In this self place where now we mean to stand.
    Hum. Here comes a man; let's stay till he be past. 12

Enter the King, with a prayer-book.

    Hen. From Scotland am I stol'n, even of pure love,
To greet mine own land with my wishful sight.
No, Harry, Harry, 'tis no land of thine;
Thy place is fill'd, thy sceptre wrung from thee,   16
Thy balm wash'd off wherewith thou was anointed:

Scene One S. d. Sinklo and Humphrey; *cf. n.*   2 laund: *glade*
4 Culling: *selecting*   9 for: *in order that*
11 self: *very*   12 stay: *postpone action*
14 wishful: *longing*   17 balm: *consecrated oil*   was: *wast*

No bending knee will call thee Cæsar now,
No humble suitors press to speak for right,
No, not a man comes for redress of thee;   20
For how can I help them, and not myself?

   Sink. Ay, here's a deer whose skin's a keeper's fee:
This is the quondam king; let's seize upon him.

   Hen. Let me embrace thee, sour adversity,   24
For wise men say it is the wisest course.

   Hum. Why linger we? let us lay hands upon him.

   Sink. Forbear awhile; we'll hear a little more.

   Hen. My queen and son are gone to France for
     aid;   28
And, as I hear, the great commanding Warwick
Is thither gone, to crave the French king's sister
To wife for Edward. If this news be true,
Poor queen and son, your labour is but lost;   32
For Warwick is a subtle orator,
And Lewis a prince soon won with moving words.
By this account then Margaret may win him,
For she's a woman to be pitied much: 36
Her sighs will make a battery in his breast;
Her tears will pierce into a marble heart;
The tiger will be mild whiles she doth mourn;
And Nero will be tainted with remorse,   40
To hear and see her plaints, her brinish tears.
Ay, but she's come to beg; Warwick, to give:
She on his left side, craving aid for Henry;
He on his right, asking a wife for Edward.   44
She weeps, and says her Henry is depos'd;
He smiles, and says his Edward is install'd;
That she, poor wretch, for grief can speak no more:
Whiles Warwick tells his title, smooths the wrong,   48

---

19 speak for right: *crave justice*   20 of: *from*
22 fee: *perquisite*   23 quondam: *one-time, former*
24 *Cf. n.*   37 battery: *bruise*   40 tainted: *touched*
47 That: *so that*   48 smooths: *glosses over*

Infereth arguments of mighty strength,
And in conclusion wins the king from her,
With promise of his sister, and what else,
To strengthen and support King Edward's place.　52
O Margaret! thus 'twill be; and thou, poor soul,
Art then forsaken, as thou went'st forlorn.

  Hum. Say, what art thou, that talk'st of kings and
    queens?

  King. More than I seem, and less than I was born
    to:　56
A man at least, for less I should not be;
And men may talk of kings, and why not I?

  Hum. Ay, but thou talk'st as if thou wert a king.

  King. Why, so I am, in mind; and that's enough.　60

  Hum. But, if thou be a king, where is thy crown?

  King. My crown is in my heart, not on my head;
Not deck'd with diamonds and Indian stones,
Nor to be seen: my crown is call'd content;　64
A crown it is that seldom kings enjoy.

  Hum. Well, if you be a king crown'd with content,
Your crown content and you must be contented
To go along with us; for, as we think,　68
You are the king King Edward hath depos'd;
And we his subjects, sworn in all allegiance,
Will apprehend you as his enemy.

  King. But did you never swear, and break an
    oath?　72

  Hum. No, never such an oath; nor will not now.

  King. Where did you dwell when I was King of
    England?

  Hum. Here in this country, where we now remain.

  King. I was anointed king at nine months old;　76
My father and my grandfather were kings,

---

50 in conclusion: *finally*　　51 what else: *anything else he desires*
57 should not: *could hardly*　　71 apprehend: *arrest*

And you were sworn true subjects unto me:
And tell me, then, have you not broke your oaths?
   Sink. No;   80
For we were subjects but while you were king.
   King. Why, am I dead? do I not breathe a man?
Ah! simple men, you know not what you swear.
Look, as I blow this feather from my face,   84
And as the air blows it to me again,
Obeying with my wind when I do blow,
And yielding to another when it blows,
Commanded always by the greater gust;   88
Such is the lightness of you common men.
But do not break your oaths; for of that sin
My mild entreaty shall not make you guilty.
Go where you will, the king shall be commanded;   92
And be you kings: command, and I'll obey.
   Sink. We are true subjects to the king, King
     Edward.
   King. So would you be again to Henry,
If he were seated as King Edward is.   96
   Sink. We charge you, in God's name and the king's,
To go with us unto the officers.
   King. In God's name, lead; your king's name be
     obey'd:
And what God will, that let your king perform;   100
And what he will, I humbly yield unto.   *Exeunt.*

Scene Two

[*London.   A Room in the Palace*]

Enter King Edward, Gloucester, Clarence, Lady Grey.

   K. Edw. Brother of Gloucester, at Saint Albans field
This lady's husband, Sir John Grey, was slain,

His lands then seiz'd on by the conqueror:
Her suit is now, to repossess those lands; 　　　4
Which we in justice cannot well deny,
Because in quarrel of the house of York
The worthy gentleman did lose his life.

   Rich. Your highness shall do well to grant her
     suit; 　　　8
It were dishonour to deny it her.

   K. Edw. It were no less: but yet I'll make a pause.

   Rich. [*Aside to Clarence.*] Yea; is it so?
I see the lady hath a thing to grant, 　　　12
Before the king will grant her humble suit.

   Clar. [*Aside to Richard.*] He knows the game: how
     true he keeps the wind!

   Rich. [*Aside to Clarence.*] Silence!

   K. Edw. Widow, we will consider of your suit, 　16
And come some other time to know our mind.

   Widow. Right gracious lord, I cannot brook delay:
May it please your highness to resolve me now,
And what your pleasure is shall satisfy me. 　　　20

   Rich. [*Aside to Clarence.*] Ay, widow? then I'll
     warrant you all your lands,
An if what pleases him shall pleasure you:
Fight closer, or, good faith, you'll catch a blow.

   Clar. [*Aside to Richard.*] I fear her not, unless she
     chance to fall. 　　　24

   Glo. [*Aside to Clarence.*] God forbid that! for he'll
     take vantages.

   K. Edw. How many children hast thou, widow? tell
     me.

   Clar. [*Aside to Richard.*] I think he means to beg
     a child of her.

6, 7 Cf. n.　　　10 pause: *delay*　　　14 wind: *advantageous position*
16 of: *concerning*　　　17 And: *and therefore*
19 resolve: *free from anxiety*　　　24 fear: *fear for*

Glo. [*Aside to Clarence.*] Nay, then, whip me; he'll
    rather give her two.   28

Widow. Three, my most gracious lord.

Glo. [*Aside to Clarence.*] You shall have four, if
    you'll be rul'd by him.

K. Edw. 'Twere pity they should lose their father's
    lands.

Widow. Be pitiful, dread lord, and grant it then.   32

K. Edw. Lords, give us leave: I'll try this widow's
    wit.

Rich. [*Aside to Clarence.*] Ay, good leave have you;
    for you will have leave,

Till youth take leave and leave you to the crutch.

                [*Retiring with Clarence.*]

K. Edw. Now, tell me, madam, do you love your
    children?   36

Widow. Ay, full as dearly as I love myself.

K. Edw. And would you not do much to do them
    good?

Widow. To do them good I would sustain some harm.

K. Edw. Then get your husband's lands, to do them
    good.   40

Widow. Therefore I came unto your majesty.

K. Edw. I'll tell you how these lands are to be got.

Widow. So shall you bind me to your highness'
    service.

K. Edw. What service wilt thou do me, if I give
    them?   44

Widow. What you command, that rests in me to do.

K. Edw. But you will take exceptions to my boon.

Widow. No, gracious lord, except I cannot do it.

K. Edw. Ay, but thou canst do what I mean to ask. 48

46 boon: *petition*

Widow. Why, then I will do what your Grace commands.

Rich. [*Aside to Clarence.*] He plies her hard; and much rain wears the marble.

Clar. [*Aside to Richard.*] As red as fire! nay, then her wax must melt.

Widow. Why stops my lord? shall I not hear my task?   52

K. Edw. An easy task: 'tis but to love a king.

Widow. That's soon perform'd, because I am a subject.

K. Edw. Why then, thy husband's lands I freely give thee.

Widow. I take my leave with many thousand thanks.   56

Rich. [*Aside to Clarence.*] The match is made; she seals it with a curtsy.

K. Edw. But stay thee; 'tis the fruits of love I mean.

Widow. The fruits of love I mean, my loving liege.

K. Edw. Ay, but, I fear me, in another sense.   60
What love think'st thou I sue so much to get?

Widow. My love till death, my humble thanks, my prayers:
That love which virtue begs and virtue grants.

K. Edw. No, by my troth, I did not mean such love.   64

Widow. Why, then you mean not as I thought you did.

K. Edw. But now you partly may perceive my mind.

Widow. My mind will never grant what I perceive
Your highness aims at, if I aim aright.   68

K. Edw. To tell thee plain, I aim to lie with thee.

68 aims at: *intends*   aim: *guess*

Widow. To tell you plain, I had rather lie in prison.

K. Edw. Why, then thou shalt not have thy husband's lands.

Widow. Why, then mine honesty shall be my dower;   72

For by that loss I will not purchase them.

K. Edw. Therein thou wrong'st thy children mightily.

Widow. Herein your highness wrongs both them and me.

But, mighty lord, this merry inclination   76
Accords not with the sadness of my suit:
Please you dismiss me, either with 'ay,' or 'no.'

K. Edw. Ay, if thou wilt say 'ay' to my request;
No, if thou dost say 'no' to my demand.   80

Widow. Then, no, my lord. My suit is at an end.

Rich. [*Aside to Clarence.*] The widow likes him not, she knits her brows.

Clar. [*Aside to Richard.*] He is the bluntest wooer in Christendom.

K. Edw. [*Aside.*] Her looks do argue her replete with modesty;   84

Her words do show her wit incomparable;
All her perfections challenge sovereignty:
One way or other, she is for a king;
And she shall be my love, or else my queen.   88
Say that King Edward take thee for his queen?

Widow. 'Tis better said than done, my gracious lord:
I am a subject fit to jest withal,
But far unfit to be a sovereign.   92

K. Edw. Sweet widow, by my state I swear to thee,
I speak no more than what my soul intends;

72 honesty: *virtue*   77 sadness: *seriousness*   84 argue: *prove*

And that is, to enjoy thee for my love.

   Widow. And that is more than I will yield unto. 96
I know I am too mean to be your queen,
And yet too good to be your concubine.

   K. Edw. You cavil, widow: I did mean, my queen.

   Widow. 'Twill grieve your Grace my sons should
     call you father. 100

   K. Edw. No more than when my daughters call thee
     mother.
Thou art a widow, and thou hast some children;
And, by God's mother, I, being but a bachelor,
Have other some: why, 'tis a happy thing 104
To be the father unto many sons.
Answer no more, for thou shalt be my queen.

   Rich. [*Aside to Clarence.*] The ghostly father now
     hath done his shrift.

   Clar. [*Aside to Richard.*] When he was made a
     shriver, 'twas for shift. 108

   K. Edw. Brothers, you muse what chat we two have
     had.

   Rich. The widow likes it not, for she looks very sad.

   K. Edw. You'd think it strange if I should marry
     her.

   Clar. To whom, my lord?

   K. Edw.   Why, Clarence, to myself. 112

   Rich. That would be ten days' wonder at the least.

   Clar. That's a day longer than a wonder lasts.

   Rich. By so much is the wonder in extremes.

   K. Edw. Well, jest on, brothers: I can tell you
     both 116
Her suit is granted for her husband's lands.

Enter a Nobleman.

104 other some: *some others*
108 for shift: *to serve a crafty purpose*   109 muse: *wonder*
114 *Cf. n.*

Nob. My gracious lord, Henry your foe is taken,
And brought as prisoner to your palace gate.

K. Edw. See that he be convey'd unto the Tower: 120
And go we, brothers, to the man that took him,
To question of his apprehension.
Widow, go you along.   Lords, use her honourably.
                              Exeunt.   Manet Richard.

Rich. Ay, Edward will use women honourably.   124
Would he were wasted, marrow, bones, and all,
That from his loins no hopeful branch may spring,
To cross me from the golden time I look for!
And yet, between my soul's desire and me—   128
The lustful Edward's title buried,—
Is Clarence, Henry, and his son young Edward,
And all the unlook'd for issue of their bodies,
To take their rooms, ere I can place myself: 132
A cold premeditation for my purpose!
Why then, I do but dream on sovereignty;
Like one that stands upon a promontory,
And spies a far-off shore where he would tread,   136
Wishing his foot were equal with his eye;
And chides the sea that sunders him from thence,
Saying, he'll lade it dry to have his way:
So do I wish the crown, being so far off,   140
And so I chide the means that keeps me from it,
And so I say I'll cut the causes off,
Flatt'ring me with impossibilities.
My eye's too quick, my heart o'erweens too much, 144
Unless my hand and strength could equal them.
Well, say there is no kingdom then for Richard;
What other pleasure can the world afford?
I'll make my heaven in a lady's lap,   148

132 rooms: *places*   133 cold premeditation: *unfavorable augury*
139 lade: *empty*   141 means: *intervening obstacles*
143 me: *myself*   144 o'erweens too much: *is too presumptuous*

And deck my body in gay ornaments,
And witch sweet ladies with my words and looks.
O miserable thought! and more unlikely
Than to accomplish twenty golden crowns. 152
Why, love forswore me in my mother's womb:
And, for I should not deal in her soft laws,
She did corrupt frail nature with some bribe,
To shrink mine arm up like a wither'd shrub; 156
To make an envious mountain on my back,
Where sits deformity to mock my body;
To shape my legs of an unequal size;
To disproportion me in every part, 160
Like to a chaos, or an unlick'd bear-whelp
That carries no impression like the dam.
And am I then a man to be belov'd?
O monstrous fault! to harbour such a thought. 164
Then, since this earth affords no joy to me
But to command, to check, to o'erbear such
As are of better person than myself,
I'll make my heaven to dream upon the crown; 168
And, whiles I live, to account this world but hell,
Until my misshap'd trunk that bears this head
Be round impaled with a glorious crown.
And yet I know not how to get the crown, 172
For many lives stand between me and home:
And I, like one lost in a thorny wood,
That rents the thorns and is rent with the thorns,
Seeking a way and straying from the way; 176
Not knowing how to find the open air,
But toiling desperately to find it out,
Torment myself to catch the English crown:
And from that torment I will free myself, 180

150 witch: *bewitch, charm*
162 carries . . . dam: *has nothing of its mother's shape; cf. n.*
166 check: *control*   171 impaled: *encircled*
173 home: *the goal*   175 rents: *tears, rends*

Or hew my way out with a bloody axe.
Why, I can smile, and murther whiles I smile,
And cry, 'Content,' to that which grieves my heart,
And wet my cheeks with artificial tears,   184
And frame my face to all occasions.
I'll drown more sailors than the mermaid shall;
I'll slay more gazers than the basilisk;
I'll play the orator as well as Nestor,   188
Deceive more slily than Ulysses could,
And, like a Sinon, take another Troy.
I can add colours to the chameleon,
Change shapes with Proteus for advantages,   192
And set the murtherous Machiavel to school.
Can I do this, and cannot get a crown?
Tut! were it farther off, I'll pluck it down.   *Exit.*

Scene Three

[Paris.   A Room in the Palace]

*Flourish.   Enter Lewis the French King, his sister
      Bona; his Admiral called Bourbon; Prince Edward,
      Queen Margaret, and the Earl of Oxford.   Lewis
      sits, and riseth up again.*

   Lew. Fair Queen of England, worthy Margaret,
Sit down with us: it ill befits thy state
And birth, that thou shouldst stand while Lewis doth
      sit.
   Mar. No, mighty King of France: now Margaret   4
Must strike her sail, and learn a while to serve
Where kings command.   I was, I must confess,

187 basilisk: *fabulous reptile whose sight was death*
191 add . . . to: *assume more colors than*
192 for advantages: *as my purpose requires*
193 *Give Machiavelli himself lessons in murder; cf. n.*
2 state: *dignity*

Great Albion's queen in former golden days;
But now mischance hath trod my title down,   8
And with dishonour laid me on the ground,
Where I must take like seat unto my fortune,
And to my humble seat conform myself.
    Lew. Why, say, fair queen, whence springs this
        deep despair?   12
    Mar. From such a cause as fills mine eyes with tears
And stops my tongue, while heart is drown'd in cares.
    Lew. Whate'er it be, be thou still like thyself,
And sit thee by our side. *Seats her by him.* Yield not
        thy neck   16
To fortune's yoke, but let thy dauntless mind
Still ride in triumph over all mischance.
Be plain, Queen Margaret, and tell thy grief;
It shall be eas'd, if France can yield relief.   20
    Mar. Those gracious words revive my drooping
        thoughts,
And give my tongue-tied sorrows leave to speak.
Now, therefore, be it known to noble Lewis,
That Henry, sole possessor of my love,   24
Is of a king become a banish'd man,
And forc'd to live in Scotland a forlorn;
While proud ambitious Edward, Duke of York,
Usurps the regal title and the seat   28
Of England's true-anointed lawful king.
This is the cause that I, poor Margaret,
With this my son, Prince Edward, Henry's heir,
Am come to crave thy just and lawful aid;   32
And if thou fail us, all our hope is done.
Scotland hath will to help, but cannot help;
Our people and our peers are both misled,
Our treasure seiz'd, our soldiers put to flight,   36

16 sit thee: *seat thyself*
25 of: *from being*
          16-18 *Cf. n.*
          26 forlorn: *outcast*

And, as thou seest, ourselves in heavy plight.

   Lew. Renowned queen, with patience calm the storm,
While we bethink a means to break it off.

   Mar. The more we stay, the stronger grows our
    foe.   40

   Lew. The more I stay, the more I'll succour thee.

   Mar. O! but impatience waiteth on true sorrow:
And see where comes the breeder of my sorrow.

Enter Warwick.

   Lew. What's he approacheth boldly to our presence?

   Mar. Our Earl of Warwick, Edward's greatest
    friend.   45

   Lew. Welcome, brave Warwick! What brings thee
    to France?

                He descends. She ariseth.

   Mar. Ay, now begins a second storm to rise;
For this is he that moves both wind and tide.   48

   War. From worthy Edward, King of Albion,
My lord and sovereign, and thy vowed friend,
I come, in kindness and unfeigned love,
First, to do greetings to thy royal person;   52
And then to crave a league of amity;
And lastly to confirm that amity
With nuptial knot, if thou vouchsafe to grant
That virtuous Lady Bona, thy fair sister,   56
To England's king in lawful marriage.

   Mar. If that go forward, Henry's hope is done.

   War. And, gracious madam,   *Speaking to Bona.*
    in our king's behalf,
I am commanded, with your leave and favour,   60
Humbly to kiss your hand, and with my tongue
To tell the passion of my sovereign's heart;

---

39 break it off: *cut it short*   42 waiteth on: *attends*
44 he: *he who*

Where fame, late entering at his heedful ears,
Hath plac'd thy beauty's image and thy virtue.   64

   Mar. King Lewis and Lady Bona, hear me speak,
Before you answer Warwick.   His demand
Springs not from Edward's well-meant honest love,
But from deceit bred by necessity;   68
For how can tyrants safely govern home,
Unless abroad they purchase great alliance?
To prove him tyrant this reason may suffice,
That Henry liveth still; but were he dead,   72
Yet here Prince Edward stands, King Henry's son.
Look, therefore, Lewis, that by this league and mar-
    riage
Thou draw not on thy danger and dishonour;
For though usurpers sway the rule awhile,   76
Yet heavens are just, and time suppresseth wrongs.

   War. Injurious Margaret!

   Prince.   And why not queen?

   War. Because thy father Henry did usurp,
And thou no more art prince than she is queen.   80

   Oxf. Then Warwick disannuls great John of Gaunt,
Which did subdue the greatest part of Spain;
And, after John of Gaunt, Henry the Fourth,
Whose wisdom was a mirror to the wisest;   84
And, after that wise prince, Henry the Fifth,
Who by his prowess conquered all France:
From these our Henry lineally descends.

   War. Oxford, how haps it, in this smooth dis-
    course,   88
You told not how Henry the Sixth hath lost
All that which Henry the Fifth had gotten?
Methinks these peers of France should smile at that.
But for the rest, you tell a pedigree   92

63 fame: *report*
81, 82 *Cf. n.*

78 Injurious: *insulting*
81 disannuls: *makes nothing of*

Of threescore and two years; a silly time
To make prescription for a kingdom's worth.

    Oxf. Why, Warwick, canst thou speak against thy
      liege,
Whom thou obeyedst thirty and six years,				96
And not bewray thy treason with a blush?

    War. Can Oxford, that did ever fence the right,
Now buckler falsehood with a pedigree?
For shame! leave Henry, and call Edward king.			100

    Oxf. Call him my king, by whose injurious doom
My elder brother, the Lord Aubrey Vere,
Was done to death? and more than so, my father,
Even in the downfall of his mellow'd years,			104
When nature brought him to the door of death?
No, Warwick, no; while life upholds this arm,
This arm upholds the house of Lancaster.

    War. And I the house of York.					108

    Lew. Queen Margaret, Prince Edward, and Oxford,
Vouchsafe at our request to stand aside,
While I use further conference with Warwick.

            They stand aloof.

    Mar. Heaven grant that Warwick's words bewitch
      him not!							112

    Lew. Now, Warwick, tell me, even upon thy con-
      science,
Is Edward your true king? for I were loath
To link with him that were not lawful chosen.

    War. Thereon I pawn my credit and mine honour.

    Lew. But is he gracious in the people's eye?			117

    War. The more that Henry was unfortunate.

    Lew. Then further, all dissembling set aside,

94 prescription: *right based on immemorial custom*   95, 96 *Cf. n.*
99 buckler: *shield, defend*   101 injurious: *unjust; cf. n.*
103 more than so: *yet more*   115 lawful: *lawfully*
118 unfortunate: *a breeder of misfortune*

Tell me for truth the measure of his love   120
Unto our sister Bona.
    War.   Such it seems
As may beseem a monarch like himself.
Myself have often heard him say and swear
That this his love was an eternal plant,   124
Whereof the root was fix'd in virtue's ground,
The leaves and fruit maintain'd with beauty's sun,
Exempt from envy, but not from disdain,
Unless the Lady Bona quit his pain.   128
    Lew. Now, sister, let us hear your firm resolve.
    Bona. Your grant, or your denial, shall be mine:
Yet I confess that often ere this day,   *Speaks to War.*
When I have heard your king's desert recounted,   132
Mine ear hath tempted judgment to desire.
    Lew. Then, Warwick, thus: our sister shall be
        Edward's;
And now forthwith shall articles be drawn
Touching the jointure that your king must make,   136
Which with her dowry shall be counterpois'd.
Draw near, Queen Margaret, and be a witness
That Bona shall be wife to the English king.
    Prince. To Edward, but not to the English king. 140
    Mar. Deceitful Warwick! it was thy device
By this alliance to make void my suit:
Before thy coming Lewis was Henry's friend.
    Lew. And still is friend to him and Margaret: 144
But if your title to the crown be weak,
As may appear by Edward's good success,
Then 'tis but reason that I be releas'd
From giving aid which late I promised.   148
Yet shall you have all kindness at my hand

127 *Cf. n.*   128 quit his pain: *requite his longing*
130 grant: *assent*   132 desert: *merit*
136 jointure: *property settled on wife at marriage*
137 counterpois'd: *equalled*

That your estate requires and mine can yield.

   War. Henry now lives in Scotland at his ease,
Where having nothing, nothing can he lose.   152
And as for you yourself, our quondam queen,
You have a father able to maintain you,
And better 'twere you troubled him than France.

   Mar. Peace! impudent and shameless Warwick,
    peace;   156
Proud setter up and puller down of kings;
I will not hence, till, with my talk and tears,
Both full of truth, I make King Lewis behold
Thy sly conveyance and thy lord's false love;   160
For both of you are birds of self-same feather.
                  Post blowing a horn within.

   Lew. Warwick, this is some post to us or thee.

Enter the Post.

   Post. My lord ambassador, these letters are for you,
                  Speaks to Warwick.
Sent from your brother, Marquess Montague: 164
These from our king unto your majesty.   *To Lewis.*
And, madam, these for you; from whom I know not.
                    To Margaret.

They all read their letters.

   Oxf. I like it well that our fair queen and mistress
Smiles at her news, while Warwick frowns at his. 168

   Prince. Nay, mark how Lewis stamps as he were
    nettled:
I hope all's for the best.

   Lew. Warwick, what are thy news? and yours, fair
    queen?

157 *Cf. n.*   160 conveyance: *deceit*
162 post: *messenger bearing letters*   169 as: *as if*

Mar. Mine, such as fill my heart with unhop'd
    joys.   172
War. Mine, full of sorrow and heart's discontent.
Lew. What! has your king married the Lady Grey?
And now, to soothe your forgery and his,
Sends me a paper to persuade me patience?   176
Is this the alliance that he seeks with France?
Dare he presume to scorn us in this manner?
    Mar. I told your majesty as much before:
This proveth Edward's love and Warwick's honesty.
    War. King Lewis, I here protest, in sight of heaven,
And by the hope I have of heavenly bliss,
That I am clear from this misdeed of Edward's;
No more my king, for he dishonours me,—   184
But most himself, if he could see his shame.
Did I forget that by the house of York
My father came untimely to his death?
Did I let pass th' abuse done to my niece?   188
Did I impale him with the regal crown?
Did I put Henry from his native right?
And am I guerdon'd at the last with shame?
Shame on himself! for my desert is honour: 192
And, to repair my honour, lost for him,
I here renounce him and return to Henry.
My noble queen, let former grudges pass,
And henceforth I am thy true servitor.   196
I will revenge his wrong to Lady Bona,
And replant Henry in his former state.
    Mar. Warwick, these words have turn'd my hate to
    love;
And I forgive and quite forget old faults,   200
And joy that thou becom'st King Henry's friend.
    War. So much his friend, ay, his unfeigned friend,

---

175 soothe your forgery: *palliate your deceit*   186, 187 *Cf. n.*
188 *Cf. n.*   190 native: *innate*   191 guerdon'd: *rewarded*

That, if King Lewis vouchsafe to furnish us
With some few bands of chosen soldiers,   204
I'll undertake to land them on our coast,
And force the tyrant from his seat by war.
'Tis not his new-made bride shall succour him:
And as for Clarence, as my letters tell me,   208
He's very likely now to fall from him,
For matching more for wanton lust than honour,
Or than for strength and safety of our country.
    Bona. Dear brother, how shall Bona be reveng'd, 212
But by thy help to this distressed queen?
    Mar. Renowned prince, how shall poor Henry live,
Unless thou rescue him from foul despair?
    Bona. My quarrel and this English queen's are
      one.   216
    War. And mine, fair Lady Bona, joins with yours.
    Lew. And mine with hers, and thine and Margaret's.
Therefore, at last, I firmly am resolv'd
You shall have aid.   220
    Mar. Let me give humble thanks for all at once.
    Lew. Then, England's messenger, return in post,
And tell false Edward, thy supposed king,
That Lewis of France is sending over masquers,   224
To revel it with him and his new bride.
Thou seest what's past; go fear thy king withal.
    Bona. Tell him, in hope he'll prove a widower
      shortly,
I wear the willow garland for his sake.   228
    Mar. Tell him, my mourning weeds are laid aside,
And I am ready to put armour on.
    War. Tell him from me, that he hath done me wrong,
And therefore I'll uncrown him ere 't be long.   232

223 supposed: *pretended*
226 what's past: *what has happened*   fear: *frighten*   withal:
    therewith   228 willow garland: *emblem of unhappy love*

There's thy reward: be gone.   *Exit Post.*
   Lew.   But, Warwick,
Thou and Oxford, with five thousand men,
Shall cross the seas, and bid false Edward battle;
And, as occasion serves, this noble queen   236
And prince shall follow with a fresh supply.
Yet ere thou go, but answer me one doubt:
What pledge have we of thy firm loyalty?
   War. This shall assure my constant loyalty: 240
That if our queen and this young prince agree,
I'll join mine eldest daughter and my joy
To him forthwith in holy wedlock bands.
   Mar. Yes, I agree, and thank you for your mo-
     tion.   244
Son Edward, she is fair and virtuous,
Therefore delay not, give thy hand to Warwick;
And, with thy hand, thy faith irrevocable,
That only Warwick's daughter shall be thine.   248
   Prince. Yes, I accept her, for she well deserves it;
And here, to pledge my vow, I give my hand.
              He gives his hand to Warwick.
   Lew. Why stay we now? These soldiers shall be
     levied,
And thou, Lord Bourbon, our high admiral,   252
Shall waft them over with our royal fleet.
I long till Edward fall by war's mischance,
For mocking marriage with a dame of France.
             Exeunt. Manet Warwick.
   War. I came from Edward as ambassador,   256
But I return his sworn and mortal foe:
Matter of marriage was the charge he gave me,
But dreadful war shall answer his demand.

---

235 bid: *offer*   242 eldest daughter; *cf. n.*   244 motion: *offer*
253 waft: *convey by water*   254 long till: *am impatient that*

Had he none else to make a stale but me?   260
Then none but I shall turn his jest to sorrow.
I was the chief that rais'd him to the crown,
And I'll be chief to bring him down again:
Not that I pity Henry's misery,   264
But seek revenge on Edward's mockery.   *Exit.*

ACT FOURTH

Scene One

[London.   A Room in the Palace]

Enter Richard, Clarence, Somerset, and Montague.

  Rich. Now tell me, brother Clarence, what think you
Of this new marriage with the Lady Grey?
Hath not our brother made a worthy choice?
  Clar. Alas! you know, 'tis far from hence to
    France;   4
How could he stay till Warwick made return?
  Som. My lords, forbear this talk; here comes the
    king.

*Flourish.   Enter King Edward, Lady Grey, Pembroke,
Stafford, Hastings.   Four stand on one side, and
four on the other.*

  Rich. And his well-chosen bride.
  Clar. I mind to tell him plainly what I think.   8
  K. Edw. Now, brother of Clarence, how like you
    our choice,
That you stand pensive, as half malcontent?
  Clar. As well as Lewis of France, or the Earl of
    Warwick,

---

260 stale: *dupe*   262 chief: *principal means*   6 S. d.; *cf. n.*
8 mind: *intend*   10 malcontent: *dissatisfied*

Which are so weak of courage and in judgment   12
That they'll take no offence at our abuse.

  K. Edw. Suppose they take offence without a cause,
They are but Lewis and Warwick: I am Edward,
Your king and Warwick's, and must have my will.   16

  Rich. And shall have your will, because our king:
Yet hasty marriage seldom proveth well.

    K. Edw. Yea, brother Richard, are you offended
      too?

  Rich. Not I: 20
No, God forbid, that I should wish them sever'd
Whom God hath join'd together; ay, and 'twere pity
To sunder them that yoke so well together.

    K. Edw. Setting your scorns and your mislike
      aside,   24
Tell me some reason why the Lady Grey
Should not become my wife and England's queen:
And you too, Somerset and Montague,
Speak freely what you think.   28

  Clar. Then this is mine opinion: that King Lewis
Becomes your enemy for mocking him
About the marriage of the Lady Bona.

  Rich. And Warwick, doing what you gave in
    charge,   32
Is now dishonoured by this new marriage.

    K. Edw. What if both Lewis and Warwick be
      appeas'd
By such invention as I can devise?

    Mont. Yet to have join'd with France in such
      alliance   36
Would more have strengthen'd this our commonwealth
'Gainst foreign storms, than any home-bred marriage.

  Hast. Why, knows not Montague, that of itself

---

13 abuse: *insult*   18 proveth: *turns out*
24 mislike: *displeasure*   35 invention: *plan*

England is safe, if true within itself?   40

   Mont. Yes; but the safer when 'tis back'd with
    France.

   Hast. 'Tis better using France than trusting France:
Let us be back'd with God and with the seas
Which he hath given for fence impregnable;   44
And with their helps only defend ourselves:
In them and in ourselves our safety lies.

   Clar. For this one speech Lord Hastings well de-
    serves

To have the heir of the Lord Hungerford.   48

   K. Edw. Ay, what of that? it was my will and grant;
And for this once my will shall stand for law.

   Rich. And yet methinks your Grace hath not done
    well,

To give the heir and daughter of Lord Scales   52
Unto the brother of your loving bride:
She better would have fitted me or Clarence:
But in your bride you bury brotherhood.

   Clar. Or else you would not have bestow'd the heir 56
Of the Lord Bonville on your new wife's son,
And leave your brothers to go speed elsewhere.

   K. Edw. Alas, poor Clarence, is it for a wife
That thou art malcontent? I will provide thee.   60

   Clar. In choosing for yourself you show'd your
    judgment,

Which being shallow, you shall give me leave
To play the broker on mine own behalf;
And to that end I shortly mind to leave you.   64

   K. Edw. Leave me, or tarry, Edward will be king,
And not be tied unto his brother's will.

   L. Grey. My lords, before it pleas'd his majesty
To raise my state to title of a queen,   68

40 *Cf. n.*   42 using: *making a tool of*
47, 48 *Cf. n.*   63 *To be my own agent*

Do me but right, and you must all confess
That I was not ignoble of descent;
And meaner than myself have had like fortune.
But as this title honours me and mine,   72
So your dislikes, to whom I would be pleasing,
Do cloud my joys with danger and with sorrow.

   K. Edw. My love, forbear to fawn upon their
    frowns:
What danger or what sorrow can befall thee,   76
So long as Edward is thy constant friend
And their true sovereign, whom they must obey?
Nay, whom they shall obey, and love thee too,
Unless they seek for hatred at my hands;   80
Which if they do, yet will I keep thee safe,
And they shall feel the vengeance of my wrath.

   Rich. [*Aside.*] I hear, yet say not much, but think
    the more.

Enter a Post.

   K. Edw. Now, messenger, what letters or what
    news   84
From France?

   Post. My sovereign liege, no letters; and few words,
But such as I, without your special pardon,
Dare not relate.   88

   K. Edw. Go to, we pardon thee: therefore, in brief,
Tell me their words as near as thou canst guess them.
What answer makes King Lewis unto our letters?

   Post. At my depart these were his very words: 92
'Go tell false Edward, thy supposed king,
That Lewis of France is sending over masquers,
To revel it with him and his new bride.'

70 not . . . descent; *cf. n.*   71 meaner: *lowlier persons*
73 your dislikes: *the displeasure of you*
75 fawn upon: *seek to propitiate*
89 Go to: *come!*   90 guess: *approximate*

K. Edw. Is Lewis so brave? belike he thinks me
  Henry.   96
But what said Lady Bona to my marriage?

Post. These were her words, utter'd with mild dis-
  dain:
'Tell him, in hope he'll prove a widower shortly,
I'll wear the willow garland for his sake.'   100

K. Edw. I blame not her, she could say little less;
She had the wrong.   But what said Henry's queen?
For I have heard that she was there in place.

Post. 'Tell him,' quoth she, 'my mourning weeds are
  done,   104
And I am ready to put armour on.'

K. Edw. Belike she minds to play the Amazon.
But what said Warwick to these injuries?

Post. He, more incens'd against your majesty   108
Than all the rest, discharg'd me with these words:
'Tell him from me that he hath done me wrong,
And therefore I'll uncrown him ere 't be long.'

K. Edw. Ha! durst the traitor breathe out so proud
  words?   112
Well, I will arm me, being thus forewarn'd:
They shall have wars, and pay for their presumption.
But say, is Warwick friends with Margaret?

Post. Ay, gracious sovereign; they are so link'd in
  friendship,   116
That young Prince Edward marries Warwick's
  daughter.

Clar. Belike the elder; Clarence will have the
  younger.
Now, brother king, farewell, and sit you fast,
For I will hence to Warwick's other daughter;   120

96 brave: *full of bravado*   103 in place: *present*
104 done: *done with, laid aside*   118 *Cf. n.*
119 sit you fast: *seat yourself firmly*

That, though I want a kingdom, yet in marriage
I may not prove inferior to yourself.
You that love me and Warwick, follow me.

               Exit Clarence, and Somerset follows.

  Rich. [*Aside.*] Not I.   124
My thoughts aim at a further matter; I
Stay not for love of Edward, but the crown.
  K. Edw. Clarence and Somerset both gone to War-
    wick!
Yet am I arm'd against the worst can happen,   128
And haste is needful in this desperate case.
Pembroke and Stafford, you in our behalf
Go levy men, and make prepare for war:
They are already, or quickly will be landed: 132
Myself in person will straight follow you.

              Exeunt Pembroke and Stafford.

But ere I go, Hastings and Montague,
Resolve my doubt   You twain, of all the rest,
Are near to Warwick by blood, and by alliance: 136
Tell me if you love Warwick more than me?
If it be so, then both depart to him;
I rather wish you foes than hollow friends:
But if you mind to hold your true obedience,   140
Give me assurance with some friendly vow
That I may never have you in suspect.
  Mont. So God help Montague as he proves true!
  Hast. And Hastings as he favours Edward's cause!
  K. Edw. Now, brother Richard, will you stand by
    us?
  Rich. Ay, in despite of all that shall withstand you.
  K. Edw. Why, so! then am I sure of victory.
Now therefore let us hence; and lose no hour   148
Till we meet Warwick with his foreign power.

                  Exeunt.

131 prepare: *preparation*   142 suspect: *suspicion*

Scene Two

[*A Plain in Warwickshire*]

Enter Warwick and Oxford in England, with French Soldiers.

War. Trust me, my lord, all hitherto goes well;
The common people by numbers swarm to us.

Enter Clarence and Somerset.

But see where Somerset and Clarence comes!
Speak suddenly, my lords, are we all friends?   4
   Clar. Fear not that, my lord.
   War. Then, gentle Clarence, welcome unto War-
     wick;
And welcome, Somerset: I hold it cowardice,
To rest mistrustful where a noble heart   8
Hath pawn'd an open hand in sign of love;
Else might I think that Clarence, Edward's brother,
Were but a feigned friend to our proceedings:
But welcome, sweet Clarence; my daughter shall be
     thine.   12
And now what rests, but in night's coverture,
Thy brother being carelessly encamp'd,
His soldiers lurking in the towns about,
And but attended by a simple guard,   16
We may surprise and take him at our pleasure?
Our scouts have found the adventure very easy:
That as Ulysses, and stout Diomede,
With sleight and manhood stole to Rhesus' tents,   20
And brought from thence the Thracian fatal steeds;
So we, well cover'd with the night's black mantle,

4 suddenly: *quickly*   5 Fear: *doubt*
13 rests: *remains to be done*   in . . . coverture: *under cover of*
   night   20 sleight: *craft*   21 Thracian . . . steeds; *cf. n.*

At unawares may beat down Edward's guard,
And seize himself; I say not, slaughter him,   24
For I intend but only to surprise him.
You, that will follow me to this attempt,
Applaud the name of Henry with your leader.
                    They all cry 'Henry!'
Why, then, let's on our way in silent sort.   28
For Warwick and his friends, God and Saint George!
                    Exeunt.

Scene Three

[Edward's Camp near Warwick]

Enter three Watchmen to guard the King's tent.

1. Watch. Come on, my masters, each man take his
    stand;
The king, by this, is set him down to sleep.
2. Watch. What, will he not to bed?
1. Watch. Why, no: for he hath made a solemn vow 4
Never to lie and take his natural rest
Till Warwick or himself be quite suppress'd.
2. Watch. To-morrow then belike shall be the day,
If Warwick be so near as men report.   8
3. Watch. But say, I pray, what nobleman is that
That with the king here resteth in his tent?
1. Watch. 'Tis the Lord Hastings, the king's chiefest
    friend.
3. Watch. O! is it so? But why commands the
    king   12
That his chief followers lodge in towns about him,
While he himself keeps in the cold field?
2. Watch. 'Tis the more honour, because the more
    dangerous.

25 surprise: *capture unawares*   28 sort: *manner*

3. Watch. Ay, but give me worship and quietness; 16
I like it better than a dangerous honour.
If Warwick knew in what estate he stands,
'Tis to be doubted he would waken him.

  1. Watch. Unless our halberds did shut up his pas-
    sage.   20
  2. Watch. Ay; wherefore else guard we his royal
    tent,
But to defend his person from night-foes?

   Enter Warwick, Clarence, Oxford, Somerset, and
       French Soldiers, silent all.

  War. This is his tent; and see where stand his
    guard.
Courage, my masters! honour now or never!   24
But follow me, and Edward shall be ours.

  1. Watch. Who goes there?
  2. Watch. Stay, or thou diest.

Warwick and the rest cry all, 'Warwick! Warwick!'
and set upon the Guard, who fly, crying, 'Arm!
Arm!' Warwick and the rest following them.

The drum playing and trumpet sounding, enter War-
  wick, Somerset, and the rest, bringing the King out
  in his gown, sitting in a chair. Richard and Hast-
  ings fly over the stage.

  Som.   What are they that fly there?
  War. Richard and Hastings: let them go; here is
    the duke.   28
  K. Edw. The duke! Why, Warwick, when we
    parted,
Thou call'dst me king!

16 worship and quietness: *honorable quiet*
18 in . . . stands: *Edward's situation*
19 doubted: *feared*   22 S. d. French Soldiers; *cf. n.*

War.   Ay, but the case is alter'd:
When you disgrac'd me in my embassade,
Then I degraded you from being king,   32
And come now to create you Duke of York.
Alas! how should you govern any kingdom,
That know not how to use ambassadors,
Nor how to be contented with one wife,   36
Nor how to use your brothers brotherly,
Nor how to study for the people's welfare,
Nor how to shroud yourself from enemies?
    K. Edw. Yea, brother of Clarence, art thou here
        too?   40
Nay, then, I see that Edward needs must down.
Yet, Warwick, in despite of all mischance,
Of thee thyself, and all thy complices,
Edward will always bear himself as king: 44
Though Fortune's malice overthrow my state,
My mind exceeds the compass of her wheel.
    War. Then, for his mind, be Edward England's
        king: *Takes off his crown.*
But Henry now shall wear the English crown,   48
And be true king indeed, thou but the shadow.
My Lord of Somerset, at my request,
See that forthwith Duke Edward be convey'd
Unto my brother, Archbishop of York.   52
When I have fought with Pembroke and his fellows,
I'll follow you, and tell what answer
Lewis and the Lady Bona send to him:
Now for a while farewell, good Duke of York.   56
                    They lead him out forcibly.
    K. Edw. What fates impose, that men must needs
        abide;

30 the case is alter'd: *conditions have changed*   39 shroud: *shelter*
43 complices: *accomplices*   47 for his mind: *in imagination*
52 *Cf. n.*   53 Pembroke; *cf. n.*

It boots not to resist both wind and tide.

    Exeunt [*Edward and Somerset, with Guard*].

 Oxf. What now remains, my lords, for us to do,

But march to London with our soldiers?   60

 War. Ay, that's the first thing that we have to do;

To free King Henry from imprisonment,

And see him seated in the regal throne.   *Exeunt.*

Scene Four

[*London. A Room in the Palace*]

Enter Rivers and Lady Grey [*Queen Elizabeth*].

 Riv. Madam, what makes you in this sudden change?

 L. Grey. Why, brother Rivers, are you yet to learn,

What late misfortune is befall'n King Edward?

 Riv. What! loss of some pitch'd battle against War-

  wick?   4

 L. Grey. No, but the loss of his own royal person.

 Riv. Then is my sovereign slain?

 L. Grey. Ay, almost slain, for he is taken prisoner;

Either betray'd by falsehood of his guard   8

Or by his foe surpris'd at unawares:

And, as I further have to understand,

Is new committed to the Bishop of York,

Fell Warwick's brother, and by that our foe.   12

 Riv. These news, I must confess, are full of grief;

Yet, gracious madam, bear it as you may:

Warwick may lose, that now hath won the day.

 L. Grey. Till then fair hope must hinder life's

  decay.   16

And I the rather wean me from despair

For love of Edward's offspring in my womb:

Scene Four; *cf. n.*   2 brother Rivers; *cf. n.*

This is it that makes me bridle passion,
And bear with mildness my misfortune's cross;   20
Ay, ay, for this I draw in many a tear,
And stop the rising of blood-sucking sighs,
Lest with my sighs or tears I blast or drown
King Edward's fruit, true heir to th' English crown. 24
 Riv. But, madam, where is Warwick then become?
 L. Grey. I am inform'd that he comes towards London,
To set the crown once more on Henry's head:
Guess thou the rest; King Edward's friends must down.   28
But, to prevent the tyrant's violence,—
For trust not him that hath once broken faith,—
I'll hence forthwith unto the sanctuary,
To save at least the heir of Edward's right: 32
There shall I rest secure from force and fraud.
Come, therefore; let us fly while we may fly:
If Warwick take us, we are sure to die.   *Exeunt.*

Scene Five

[*A Park near Middleham Castle in Yorkshire*]

Enter Richard, Lord Hastings, and Sir William Stanley.

 Rich. Now, my Lord Hastings and Sir William Stanley,
Leave off to wonder why I drew you hither,
Into this chiefest thicket of the park.   3
Thus stands the case. You know, our king, my brother,
Is prisoner to the bishop here, at whose hands

22 blood-sucking sighs; *cf. n.*   31, 32 *Cf. n.*
Scene Five; *cf. n.*

He hath good usage and great liberty,
And often but attended with weak guard,
Comes hunting this way to disport himself.   8
I have advertis'd him by secret means,
That if about this hour he make this way,
Under the colour of his usual game,
He shall here find his friends, with horse and men   12
To set him free from his captivity.

Enter King Edward, and a Huntsman with him.

  Hunt. This way, my lord, for this way lies the
    game.
  K. Edw. Nay, this way, man: see where the hunts-
    men stand.
Now, brother of Gloucester, Lord Hastings, and the
    rest,   16
Stand you thus close, to steal the bishop's deer?
  Rich. Brother, the time and case requireth haste.
Your horse stands ready at the park corner.
  K. Edw. But whither shall we then?   20
  Hast. To Lynn, my lord; and, shipp'd, from thence
    to Flanders.
  Rich. Well guess'd, believe me; for that was my
    meaning.
  K. Edw. Stanley, I will requite thy forwardness.
  Rich. But wherefore stay we? 'tis no time to talk. 24
  K. Edw. Huntsman, what sayst thou? wilt thou go
    along?
  Hunt. Better do so than tarry and be hang'd.
  Rich. Come then, away; let's ha' no more ado.
  K. Edw. Bishop, farewell: shield thee from War-
    wick's frown,
And pray that I may repossess the crown.   *Exeunt.*

17 close: *in concealment*

Scene Six

[A Room in the Tower]

Flourish.   Enter King Henry the Sixth, Clarence, Warwick, Somerset, young Henry [Earl of Richmond], Oxford, Montague, and Lieutenant [of the Tower].

K. Hen. Master lieutenant, now that God and friends
Have shaken Edward from the regal seat,
And turn'd my captive state to liberty,
My fear to hope, my sorrows unto joys,   4
At our enlargement what are thy due fees?

   Lieu. Subjects may challenge nothing of their
      sovereigns;
But if a humble prayer may prevail,
I then crave pardon of your majesty.   8

   K. Hen. For what, lieutenant? for well using me?
Nay, be thou sure, I'll well requite thy kindness,
For that it made my imprisonment a pleasure;
Ay, such a pleasure as encaged birds   12
Conceive, when, after many moody thoughts
At last by notes of household harmony
They quite forget their loss of liberty.
But, Warwick, after God, thou set'st me free, 16
And chiefly therefore I thank God and thee;
He was the author, thou the instrument.
Therefore, that I may conquer Fortune's spite
By living low, where Fortune cannot hurt me,   20
And that the people of this blessed land
May not be punish'd with my thwarting stars,
Warwick, although my head still wear the crown,

5 enlargement: *liberation*
14 notes . . . harmony: *filling the house with song*
22 with . . . stars: *by my bad luck*

I here resign my government to thee,   24
For thou art fortunate in all thy deeds.

   War. Your Grace hath still been fam'd for virtuous;
And now may seem as wise as virtuous,
By spying and avoiding Fortune's malice;   28
For few men rightly temper with the stars:
Yet in this one thing let me blame your Grace,
For choosing me when Clarence is in place.

   Clar. No, Warwick, thou art worthy of the sway,   32
To whom the heavens, in thy nativity
Adjudg'd an olive branch and laurel crown,
As likely to be blest in peace and war;
And therefore I yield thee my free consent.   36

   War. And I choose Clarence only for protector.

   K. Hen. Warwick and Clarence, give me both your
     hands:
Now join your hands, and with your hands your
     hearts,
That no dissension hinder government: 40
I make you both protectors of this land,
While I myself will lead a private life,
And in devotion spend my latter days,
To sin's rebuke and my Creator's praise.   44

   War. What answers Clarence to his sovereign's will?

   Clar. That he consents, if Warwick yield consent;
For on thy fortune I repose myself.

   War. Why then, though loath, yet must I be con-
     tent: 48
We'll yoke together, like a double shadow
To Henry's body, and supply his place;
I mean, in bearing weight of government,
While he enjoys the honour and his ease.   52
And, Clarence, now then it is more than needful

---

29 temper: *work in harmony*

Forthwith that Edward be pronounc'd a traitor,
And all his lands and goods be confiscate.

   Clar. What else? and that succession be deter-
     min'd.   56

   War. Ay, therein Clarence shall not want his part.

   K. Hen. But, with the first of all your chief affairs,
Let me entreat, for I command no more,
That Margaret your queen, and my son Edward,   60
Be sent for, to return from France with speed:
For, till I see them here, by doubtful fear
My joy of liberty is half eclips'd.

   Clar. It shall be done, my sovereign, with all
     speed.   64

   K. Hen. My Lord of Somerset, what youth is that,
Of whom you seem to have so tender care?

   Som. My liege, it is young Henry, Earl of Rich-
     mond.

   K. Hen. Come hither, England's hope.
             Lays his hand on his head.

                        If secret powers 68
Suggest but truth to my divining thoughts,
This pretty lad will prove our country's bliss.
His looks are full of peaceful majesty,
His head by nature fram'd to wear a crown,   72
His hand to wield a sceptre, and himself
Likely in time to bless a regal throne.
Make much of him, my lords; for this is he
Must help you more than you are hurt by me.   76

               Enter a Post.

   War. What news, my friend?

   Post. That Edward is escaped from your brother,
And fled, as he hears since, to Burgundy.

67 Henry, Earl of Richmond; *cf. n.*

War. Unsavoury news! but how made he escape?   80
Post. He was convey'd by Richard, Duke of Glouces-
ter,
And the Lord Hastings, who attended him
In secret ambush on the forest side,
And from the bishop's huntsmen rescu'd him: 84
For hunting was his daily exercise.
War. My brother was too careless of his charge.
But let us hence, my sovereign, to provide
A salve for any sore that may betide.   88
                    Exeunt.   Mane[n]t Somerset, Richmond,
                                            and Oxford.
Som. My lord, I like not of this flight of Edward's;
For doubtless Burgundy will yield him help,
And we shall have more wars before 't be long.
As Henry's late presaging prophecy   92
Did glad my heart with hope of this young Richmond,
So doth my heart misgive me, in these conflicts
What may befall him to his harm and ours:
Therefore, Lord Oxford, to prevent the worst,   96
Forthwith we'll send him hence to Brittany,
Till storms be past of civil enmity.
Oxf. Ay, for if Edward repossess the crown,
'Tis like that Richmond with the rest shall down. 100
Som. It shall be so; he shall to Brittany.
Come, therefore, let's about it speedily.   *Exeunt.*

81 convey'd: *stolen away*   82 attended: *awaited*
88 betide: *chance, happen*   89 like not of: *am troubled by*

Scene Seven

[Before York]

Flourish.   Enter Edward, Richard, Hastings, and
Soldiers.

K. Edw. Now, brother Richard, Lord Hastings, and
the rest,
Yet thus far Fortune maketh us amends,
And says that once more I shall interchange
My waned state for Henry's regal crown.   4
Well have we pass'd, and now repass'd the seas,
And brought desired help from Burgundy:
What then remains, we being thus arriv'd
From Ravenspurgh haven before the gates of York,   8
But that we enter, as into our dukedom?
   Rich. The gates made fast! Brother, I like not this;
For many men that stumble at the threshold
Are well foretold that danger lurks within.   12
   K. Edw. Tush, man! abodements must not now
affright us.
By fair or foul means we must enter in,
For hither will our friends repair to us.
   Hast. My liege, I'll knock once more to summon
them.   16

Enter, on the Walls, the Mayor of York and his
Brethren.

   May. My lords, we were forewarned of your coming,
And shut the gates for safety of ourselves;
For now we owe allegiance unto Henry.
   K. Edw. But, Master Mayor, if Henry be your
king,   20

Scene Seven; *cf. n.*   8 Ravenspurgh; *cf. n.*
12 foretold: *forewarned*   13 abodements: *omens*

Yet Edward, at the least, is Duke of York.

    May. True, my good lord, I know you for no less.

    K. Edw. Why, and I challenge nothing but my duke-
    dom,

As being well content with that alone.   24

    Rich. [*Aside.*] But when the fox hath once got in
    his nose,

He'll soon find means to make the body follow.

    Hast. Why, Master Mayor, why stand you in a
    doubt?

Open the gates; we are King Henry's friends.   28

    May. Ay, say you so? the gates shall then be open'd.
                              He descends.

    Rich. A wise stout captain, and soon persuaded.

    Hast. The good old man would fain that all were
    well,

So 'twere not long of him; but being enter'd,   32

I doubt not, I, but we shall soon persuade

Both him and all his brothers unto reason.

        Enter the Mayor and two Aldermen.

    K. Edw. So, Master Mayor: these gates must not be
    shut

But in the night, or in the time of war.   36

What! fear not, man, but yield me up the keys;
                               Takes his keys.

For Edward will defend the town and thee,

And all those friends that deign to follow me.

    March.   *Enter Montgomery with drum and Soldiers.*

    Rich. Brother, this is Sir John Montgomery,   40

Our trusty friend, unless I be deceiv'd.

---

23 challenge: *claim*   32 long of: *on account of*
40 Sir John Montgomery; *cf. n.*

K. Edw. Welcome, Sir John! but why come you in
    arms?

Mont. To help King Edward in his time of storm,
As every loyal subject ought to do.   44

K. Edw. Thanks, good Montgomery; but we now
    forget
Our title to the crown, and only claim
Our dukedom till God please to send the rest.

Mont. Then fare you well, for I will hence again: 48
I came to serve a king and not a duke.
Drummer, strike up, and let us march away.

                          The drum begins to march.

K. Edw. Nay, stay, Sir John, awhile; and we'll
    debate
By what safe means the crown may be recover'd.   52

Mont. What talk you of debating? in few words,
If you'll not here proclaim yourself our king,
I'll leave you to your fortune, and be gone
To keep them back that come to succour you.   56
Why shall we fight, if you pretend no title?

Rich. Why, brother, wherefore stand you on nice
    points?

K. Edw. When we grow stronger then we'll make
    our claim;
Till then, 'tis wisdom to conceal our meaning.   60

Hast. Away with scrupulous wit! now arms must
    rule.

Rich. And fearless minds climb soonest unto crowns.
Brother, we will proclaim you out of hand;
The bruit thereof will bring you many friends.   64

K. Edw. Then be it as you will; for 'tis my right,
And Henry but usurps the diadem.

50 Drummer; *cf. n.*   50 S. d. march: *sound signal for marching*
58 stand . . . points: *boggle over technicalities*
61 scrupulous wit: *cautious calculation*
63 out of hand: *at once*   64 bruit: *rumor*

Mont. Ay, now my sovereign speaketh like himself;
And now will I be Edward's champion.   68

   Hast. Sound, trumpet!   Edward shall be here pro-
      claim'd;
Come, fellow soldier, make thou proclamation.

Flourish.   Sound.

   Sold. Edward the Fourth, by the grace of
God, King of England and France, and Lord 72
of Ireland, &c.

   Mont. And whosoe'er gainsays King Edward's
      right,
By this I challenge him to single fight.

Throws down his gauntlet.

   All. Long live Edward the Fourth!   76

   K. Edw. Thanks, brave Montgomery;—and thanks
      unto you all:
If Fortune serve me, I'll requite this kindness.
Now, for this night, let's harbour here in York;
And when the morning sun shall raise his car   80
Above the border of this horizon,
We'll forward towards Warwick, and his mates;
For well I wot that Henry is no soldier.
Ah, froward Clarence, how evil it beseems thee   84
To flatter Henry, and forsake thy brother!
Yet, as we may, we'll meet both thee and Warwick.
Come on, brave soldiers: doubt not of the day;
And, that once gotten, doubt not of large pay.   88

Exeunt.

80 car: *chariot of Phœbus*   84 evil: *ill*
85 flatter: *serve obsequiously*

Scene Eight

[*London.　A Room in the Bishop of London's Palace*]

*Flourish.　Enter the King [Henry], Warwick, Mon-
tague, Clarence, Oxford, and Exeter.*

War. What counsel, lords?　Edward from Belgia,
With hasty Germans and blunt Hollanders,
Hath pass'd in safety through the narrow seas,
And with his troops doth march amain to London;　4
And many giddy people flock to him.
　King. Let's levy men, and beat him back again.
　Clar. A little fire is quickly trodden out,
Which, being suffer'd, rivers cannot quench.　8
　War. In Warwickshire I have true-hearted friends,
Not mutinous in peace, yet bold in war;
Those will I muster up: and thou, son Clarence,
Shalt stir up in Suffolk, Norfolk, and in Kent,　12
The knights and gentlemen to come with thee:
Thou, brother Montague, in Buckingham,
Northampton, and in Leicestershire, shalt find
Men well inclin'd to hear what thou command'st:　16
And thou, brave Oxford, wondrous well belov'd,
In Oxfordshire shalt muster up thy friends.
My sovereign, with the loving citizens,
Like to his island girt in with the ocean,　20
Or modest Dian circled with her nymphs,
Shall rest in London till we come to him.
Fair lords, take leave, and stand not to reply.
Farewell, my sovereign.　24
　K. Hen. Farewell, my Hector, and my Troy's true
　　hope.

Scene Eight S. d. Exeter; *cf. n.*　　　　8 suffer'd: *ignored*
23 stand: *delay*

Clar. In sign of truth, I kiss your highness' hand.

K. Hen. Well-minded Clarence, be thou fortunate!

Mont. Comfort, my lord; and so, I take my leave.   28

Oxf. [*Kissing Henry's hand.*] And thus I seal my
    truth, and bid adieu.

K. Hen. Sweet Oxford, and my loving Montague,
And all at once, once more a happy farewell.   31

War. Farewell, sweet lords: let's meet at Coventry.

            Exeunt [*all but King Henry and Exeter*].

K. Hen. Here at the palace will I rest awhile.
Cousin of Exeter, what thinks your lordship?
Methinks the power that Edward hath in field
Should not be able to encounter mine.   36

Exe. The doubt is that he will seduce the rest.

K. Hen. That's not my fear; my meed hath got me
    fame:
I have not stopp'd mine ears to their demands,
Nor posted off their suits with slow delays;   40
My pity hath been balm to heal their wounds,
My mildness hath allay'd their swelling griefs,
My mercy dried their water-flowing tears;
I have not been desirous of their wealth;   44
Nor much oppress'd them with great subsidies,
Nor forward of revenge, though they much err'd.
Then why should they love Edward more than me?
No, Exeter, these graces challenge grace: 48
And when the lion fawns upon the lamb,
The lamb will never cease to follow him.

        Shout within, 'A Lancaster! A Lancaster!'

Exe. Hark, hark, my lord! what shouts are these?

    Enter Edward, [Richard,] and his Soldiers.

31 at once: *together*   37 doubt: *fear*   38 meed: *merit*
40 posted off: *carelessly postponed*
45 subsidies: *taxes*
46 forward of: (*been*) *eager for*   50 S. d. A Lancaster; *cf. n.*

K. Edw. Seize on the shamefac'd Henry! bear him
　　hence:　　　　　　　　　　　　　　　　52
And once again proclaim us King of England.
You are the fount that makes small brooks to flow:
Now stops thy spring, my sea shall suck them dry,
And swell so much the higher by their ebb.　　　56
Hence with him to the Tower! let him not speak.
　　　　　　Exit [Attendant] with King Henry.
And, lords, towards Coventry bend we our course,
Where peremptory Warwick now remains:
The sun shines hot, and if we use delay,　　　　60
Cold biting winter mars our hop'd-for hay.

　Rich. Away betimes, before his forces join,
And take the great-grown traitor unawares:
Brave warriors, march amain towards Coventry.　64
　　　　　　　　　　　　　　　　Exeunt.

ACT FIFTH

Scene One

[Coventry]

Enter Warwick, the Mayor of Coventry, two Mes-
　sengers, and others, upon the Walls.

　War. Where is the post that came from valiant
　　Oxford?
How far hence is thy lord, mine honest fellow?
　1. Mess. By this at Dunsmore, marching hitherward.
　War. How far off is our brother Montague?　　4
Where is the post that came from Montague?

52 shamefac'd: *shamefast, bashful*
55 Now . . . spring: *now that your spring is stopped*
60, 61 *Cf. n.*
3 Dunsmore: *Dunsmore Heath, eight miles east of Coventry*

2. Mess. By this at Daintry, with a puissant troop.

Enter [Sir John] Somerville.

War. Say, Somerville, what says my loving son?
And, by thy guess, how nigh is Clarence now?   8
    Som. At Southam I did leave him with his forces,
And do expect him here some two hours hence.

                                            [*Drum heard.*]

    War. Then Clarence is at hand. I hear his drum.
    Som. It is not his, my lord; here Southam lies: 12
The drum your honour hears marcheth from Warwick.
    War. Who should that be? belike, unlook'd for
        friends.
    Som. They are at hand, and you shall quickly know.

March.   Flourish.   Enter Edward, Richard, and
Soldiers.

    K. Edw. Go, trumpet, to the walls, and sound a
        parle.   16
    Rich. See how the surly Warwick mans the wall.
    War. O, unbid spite! is sportful Edward come?
Where slept our scouts, or how are they seduc'd,
That we could hear no news of his repair?   20
    K. Edw. Now, Warwick, wilt thou ope the city
        gates,
Speak gentle words, and humbly bend thy knee?—
Call Edward king, and at his hands beg mercy?
And he shall pardon thee these outrages.   24
    War. Nay, rather, wilt thou draw thy forces
        hence,—
Confess who set thee up and pluck'd thee down?—
Call Warwick patron, and be penitent;
And thou shalt still remain the Duke of York.   28

6 Daintry: *Daventry, 20 miles southeast*   9 Southam: *15 miles south*
13 Warwick: *12 miles southwest*   16 parle: *parley*
18 unbid: *unwelcome*   20 repair: *approach*

Rich. I thought, at least he would have said the
   king;
Or did he make the jest against his will?

War. Is not a dukedom, sir, a goodly gift?

Rich. Ay, by my faith, for a poor earl to g.ve: 32
I'll do thee service for so good a gift.

War. 'Twas I that gave the kingdom to thy brother.

K. Edw. Why then 'tis mine, if but by Warwick's
   gift.

War. Thou art no Atlas for so great a weight: 36
And, weakling, Warwick takes his gift again;
And Henry is my king, Warwick his subject.

K. Edw. But Warwick's king is Edward's prisoner;
And, gallant Warwick, do but answer this,   40
What is the body, when the head is off?

Rich. Alas! that Warwick had no more forecast,
But, whiles he thought to steal the single ten,
The king was slily finger'd from the deck.   44
You left poor Henry at the bishop's palace,
And, ten to one, you'll meet him in the Tower.

K. Edw. 'Tis even so: yet you are Warwick still.

Rich. Come, Warwick, take the time; kneel down,
   kneel down: 48
Nay, when! strike now, or else the iron cools.

War. I had rather chop this hand off at a blow,
And with the other fling it at thy face,
Than bear so low a sail to strike to thee.   52

K. Edw. Sail how thou canst, have wind and tide
   thy friend;
This hand, fast wound about thy coal-black hair,
Shall, whiles thy head is warm and new cut off,
Write in the dust this sentence with thy blood: 56

36 Atlas: *capable supporter*
43 single: *simple, unimportant*
45 bishop's palace; *cf. n.*
49 Nay, when: *come! come!*

42 forecast: *forethought*
44 deck: *pack of cards*
48 time: *favorable moment*

'Wind-changing Warwick now can change no more.'

Enter Oxford, with drum and colours.

War. O cheerful colours! see where Oxford comes!
Oxf. Oxford, Oxford, for Lancaster!
      [*He and his Forces enter the city.*]
Rich. The gates are open, let us enter too.   60
K. Edw. So other foes may set upon our backs.
Stand we in good array; for they no doubt
Will issue out again and bid us battle:
If not, the city being but of small defence,   64
We'll quickly rouse the traitors in the same.

War. O! welcome, Oxford! for we want thy help.

Enter Montague, with drum and colours.

Mont. Montague, Montague, for Lancaster!
      [*He and his Forces enter the city.*]
Rich. Thou and thy brother both shall buy this
  treason   68
Even with the dearest blood your bodies bear.

K. Edw. The harder match'd, the greater victory:
My mind presageth happy gain, and conquest.

Enter Somerset, with drum and colours.

Som. Somerset, Somerset, for Lancaster!   72
      [*He and his Forces enter the city.*]
Rich. Two of thy name, both Dukes of Somerset,
Have sold their lives unto the house of York;
And thou shalt be the third, if this sword hold.

Enter Clarence, with drum and colours.

War. And lo! where George of Clarence sweeps
  along,   76
Of force enough to bid his brother battle;

57 Wind-changing: *fickle as the wind*   63 bid: *offer*
64 of small defence: *ill-fortified*   73 Two of thy name; *cf. n.*

With whom an upright zeal to right prevails
More than the nature of a brother's love.
Come, Clarence, come; thou wilt, if Warwick call. 80
  Clar. Father of Warwick, know you what this
    means?

          [*Taking the red rose out of his helmet.*]
Look here, I throw my infamy at thee:
I will not ruinate my father's house,
Who gave his blood to lime the stones together, 84
And set up Lancaster. Why, trow'st thou, Warwick,
That Clarence is so harsh, so blunt, unnatural,
To bend the fatal instruments of war
Against his brother and his lawful king? 88
Perhaps thou wilt object my holy oath:
To keep that oath were more impiety
Than Jephthah's, when he sacrific'd his daughter.
I am so sorry for my trespass made 92
That, to deserve well at my brother's hands,
I here proclaim myself thy mortal foe;
With resolution, wheresoe'er I meet thee—
As I will meet thee if thou stir abroad— 96
To plague thee for thy foul misleading me.
And so, proud-hearted Warwick, I defy thee,
And to my brother turn my blushing cheeks.
Pardon me, Edward, I will make amends; 100
And, Richard, do not frown upon my faults,
For I will henceforth be no more unconstant.
  K. Edw. Now welcome more, and ten times more
    belov'd,
Than if thou never hadst deserv'd our hate. 104
  Rich. Welcome, good Clarence; this is brotherlike.
  War. O passing traitor, perjur'd, and unjust!

78 to: *for*   81 S. d.; *cf. n.*
84 lime: *cement*   89 object: *urge*
92 my trespass made: *the fault I have already committed*
106 passing: *surpassing*

    K. Edw. What, Warwick, wilt thou leave the town,
       and fight?

Or shall we beat the stones about thine ears?   108

    War. Alas! I am not coop'd here for defence:

I will away towards Barnet presently,

And bid thee battle, Edward, if thou dar'st.

    K. Edw. Yes, Warwick, Edward dares, and leads
       the way.   112

Lords, to the field; Saint George and victory! *Exeunt.*
        March. Warwick and his company follows.

Scene Two

[A Field of Battle near Barnet]

*Alarum and Excursions. Enter Edward, bringing
        forth Warwick, wounded.*

    K. Edw. So, lie thou there: die thou, and die our
       fear;

For Warwick was a bug that fear'd us all.

Now Montague, sit fast; I seek for thee,

That Warwick's bones may keep thine company.   4
           Exit.

    War. Ah! who is nigh? come to me, friend or foe,

And tell me who is victor, York or Warwick?

Why ask I that? my mangled body shows,

My blood, my want of strength, my sick heart shows, 8

That I must yield my body to the earth,

And, by my fall, the conquest to my foe.

Thus yields the cedar to the axe's edge,

Whose arms gave shelter to the princely eagle,   12

Under whose shade the ramping lion slept,

109 Alas: *forsooth*   2 bug: *imaginary terror*
13 ramping: *rampant, fierce*

Whose top branch overpeer'd Jove's spreading tree,
And kept low shrubs from winter's powerful wind.
These eyes, that now are dimm'd with death's black
　　veil,　　　　　　　　　　　　　　　　16
Have been as piercing as the mid-day sun,
To search the secret treasons of the world:
The wrinkles in my brows, now fill'd with blood,
Were liken'd oft to kingly sepulchres;　　　　20
For who liv'd king, but I could dig his grave?
And who durst smile when Warwick bent his brow?
Lo! now my glory smear'd in dust and blood;
My parks, my walks, my manors that I had,　　24
Even now forsake me; and of all my lands
Is nothing left me but my body's length.
Why, what is pomp, rule, reign, but earth and dust?
And, live we how we can, yet die we must.　　28

Enter Oxford and Somerset.

Som. Ah! Warwick, Warwick, wert thou as we are,
We might recover all our loss again.
The queen from France hath brought a puissant power;
Even now we heard the news.　Ah, couldst thou fly! 32
War. Why, then, I would not fly.　Ah! Montague,
If thou be there, sweet brother, take my hand,
And with thy lips keep in my soul awhile.
Thou lov'st me not; for, brother, if thou didst,　36
Thy tears would wash this cold congealed blood
That glues my lips and will not let me speak.
Come quickly, Montague, or I am dead.
Som. Ah! Warwick, Montague hath breath'd his
　　last;　　　　　　　　　　　　　　　　40
And to the latest gasp, cried out for Warwick,
And said, 'Commend me to my valiant brother.'

14 overpeer'd . . . tree: *towered above the oak*
23 smear'd: *is soiled*　　　　　　　　　31 *Cf. n.*

And more he would have said; and more he spoke,
Which sounded like a clamour in a vault,   44
That mought not be distinguish'd: but at last
I well might hear, deliver'd with a groan,
'O! farewell, Warwick!'

 War. Sweet rest his soul! Fly, lords, and save your-
  selves;   48
For Warwick bids you all farewell, to meet in heaven.
            [Dies.]

 Oxf. Away, away, to meet the queen's great power.
   Here they bear away his body. Exeunt.

Scene Three

[Another Part of the Field]

*Flourish.   Enter King Edward, in triumph: with
  Richard, Clarence, and the rest.*

 K. Edw. Thus far our fortune keeps an upward
  course,
And we are grac'd with wreaths of victory.
But in the midst of this bright-shining day,
I spy a black, suspicious, threat'ning cloud,   4
That will encounter with our glorious sun,
Ere he attain his easeful western bed:
I mean, my lords, those powers that the queen
Hath rais'd in Gallia have arriv'd our coast,   8
And, as we hear, march on to fight with us.

 Clar. A little gale will soon disperse that cloud,
And blow it to the source from whence it came:
Thy very beams will dry those vapours up,   12
For every cloud engenders not a storm.

 Rich. The queen is valu'd thirty thousand strong,

50 S. d.; *cf. n.*   8 arriv'd: *landed at*

And Somerset, with Oxford, fled to her:
If she have time to breathe, be well assur'd   16
Her faction will be full as strong as ours.

  K. Edw. We are advertis'd by our loving friends
That they do hold their course toward Tewkesbury.
We, having now the best at Barnet field,   20
Will thither straight, for willingness rids way;
And, as we march, our strength will be augmented
In every county as we go along.
Strike up the drum! cry 'Courage!' and away.   24

                                        Exeunt.

Scene Four

[*Plains near Tewkesbury*]

Flourish.   March.   Enter the Queen, young Edward,
       Somerset, Oxford, and Soldiers.

  Queen. Great lords, wise men ne'er sit and wail their
       loss,
But cheerly seek how to redress their harms.
What though the mast be now blown overboard,
The cable broke, the holding anchor lost,   4
And half our sailors swallow'd in the flood?
Yet lives our pilot still: is 't meet that he
Should leave the helm and like a fearful lad
With tearful eyes add water to the sea,   8
And give more strength to that which hath too much;
Whiles in his moan the ship splits on the rock,
Which industry and courage might have sav'd?
Ah, what a shame! ah, what a fault were this!   12
Say, Warwick was our anchor; what of that?
And Montague our top-mast; what of him?

21 rids way: *does away with distance*   1-38 *Cf. n.*
2 cheerly: *blithely*

Our slaughter'd friends the tackles; what of these?
Why, is not Oxford here another anchor?   16
And Somerset another goodly mast?
The friends of France our shrouds and tacklings?
And, though unskilful, why not Ned and I
For once allow'd the skilful pilot's charge?   20
We will not from the helm, to sit and weep,
But keep our course, though the rough wind say no,
From shelves and rocks that threaten us with wrack.
As good to chide the waves as speak them fair.   24
And what is Edward but a ruthless sea?
What Clarence but a quicksand of deceit?
And Richard but a ragged fatal rock?
All those the enemies to our poor bark.   28
Say you can swim; alas! 'tis but a while:
Tread on the sand; why, there you quickly sink:
Bestride the rock; the tide will wash you off,
Or else you famish; that's a threefold death.   32
This speak I, lords, to let you understand,
If case some one of you would fly from us,
That there's no hop'd-for mercy with the brothers
More   than   with   ruthless   waves,   with   sands   and
        rocks.
Why, courage, then! what cannot be avoided
'Twere childish weakness to lament or fear.

    Prince. Methinks a woman of this valiant spirit
Should, if a coward heard her speak these words,   40
Infuse his breast with magnanimity,
And make him, naked, foil a man at arms.
I speak not this, as doubting any here;
For did I but suspect a fearful man,   44
He should have leave to go away betimes,

---

15 tackles: *ropes*   23 shelves: *sandbanks*
27 ragged: *jagged*   34 If case: *if it should happen*
41 magnanimity: *courage*

Lest in our need he might infect another,
And make him of like spirit to himself.
If any such be here, as God forbid!   **48**
Let him depart before we need his help.

Oxf. Women and children of so high a courage,
And warriors faint! why, 'twere perpetual shame.
O brave young prince! thy famous grandfather   **52**
Doth live again in thee: long mayst thou live
To bear his image and renew his glories!

Som. And he, that will not fight for such a hope,
Go home to bed, and, like the owl by day,   **56**
If he arise, be mock'd and wonder'd at.

Queen. Thanks, gentle Somerset: sweet **Oxford**,
    thanks.

Prince. And take his thanks that yet hath nothing
    else.

Enter a Messenger.

Mess. Prepare you, lords, for Edward is at hand, **60**
Ready to fight; therefore be resolute.

Oxf. I thought no less: it is his policy
To haste thus fast, to find us unprovided.

Som. But he's deceiv'd; we are in readiness.   **64**

Queen. This cheers my heart to see your forward-
    ness.

Oxf. Here pitch our battle; hence we will not budge.

Flourish, and march.   Enter Edward, Richard,
    Clarence, and Soldiers.

K. Edw. Brave followers, yonder stands the thorny
    wood,   **67**
Which, by the heavens' assistance and your strength,
Must by the roots be hewn up yet ere night.
I need not add more fuel to your fire,

63 unprovided: *unprepared*

For well I wot ye blaze to burn them out:
Give signal to the fight, and to it, lords.   72

    Queen. Lords, knights, and gentlemen, what I should say
My tears gainsay; for every word I speak,
Ye see, I drink the water of my eye.
Therefore, no more but this: Henry, your sovereign, 76
Is prisoner to the foe; his state usurp'd,
His realm a slaughter house, his subjects slain,
His statutes cancell'd, and his treasure spent;
And yonder is the wolf that makes this spoil.   80
You fight in justice: then, in God's name, lords,
Be valiant, and give signal to the fight.   *Exeunt.*
                  Alarum. Retreat. Excursions.

Scene Five

[*Another Part of the Same*]

*Flourish.   Enter Edward, Richard, Clarence [with]
    Queen, Oxford, Somerset [as prisoners].*

    K. Edw. Now, here a period of tumultuous broils.
Away with Oxford to Hames Castle straight:
For Somerset, off with his guilty head.
Go, bear them hence; I will not hear them speak.   4
    Oxf. For my part, I'll not trouble thee with words.
    Som. Nor I, but stoop with patience to my fortune.
                    Exeunt [guarded].
    Queen. So part we sadly in this troublous world,
To meet with joy in sweet Jerusalem.   8
    K. Edw. Is proclamation made, that who finds Edward

---

74 gainsay: *forbid*   82 S. d. Excursions: *sallies across the stage*
1 period: *full stop*   2 Hames Castle; *cf. n.*

Shall have a high reward, and he his life?

Rich. It is: and lo, where youthful Edward comes.

Enter the Prince [led in by Soldiers].

K. Edw. Bring forth the gallant: let us hear him
    speak.   12

What! can so young a thorn begin to prick?

Edward, what satisfaction canst thou make,

For bearing arms, for stirring up my subjects,

And all the trouble thou hast turn'd me to?   16

Prince. Speak like a subject, proud ambitious York!

Suppose that I am now my father's mouth:

Resign thy chair, and where I stand kneel thou,

Whilst I propose the self-same words to thee,   20

Which, traitor, thou wouldst have me answer to.

Queen. Ah, that thy father had been so resolv'd!

Rich. That you might still have worn the petticoat,

And ne'er have stol'n the breech from Lancaster.   24

Prince. Let Æsop fable in a winter's night;

His currish riddles sorts not with this place.

Rich. By heaven, brat, I'll plague ye for that word.

Queen. Ay, thou wast born to be a plague to men. 28

Rich. For God's sake, take away this captive scold.

Prince. Nay, take away this scolding crookback
    rather.

K. Edw. Peace, wilful boy, or I will charm your
    tongue.

Clar. Untutor'd lad, thou art too malapert.   32

Prince. I know my duty; you are all undutiful:

Lascivious Edward, and thou perjur'd George,

And thou misshapen Dick, I tell ye all,

I am your better, traitors as ye are;   36

18 mouth: *representative*   24 breech: *breeches*
25 Æsop; *cf. n.*   26 sorts: *agree*
31 charm: *silence*   32 malapert: *impudent*

And thou usurp'st my father's right and mine.

 K. Edw. Take that, the likeness of this railer here.

           Stabs him.

 Rich. Sprawl'st thou? take that, to end thy agony.

           Rich. stabs him.

 Clar. And there's for twitting me with perjury. 40

           Clar. stabs him.

 Queen. O, kill me too!

 Rich. Marry, and shall.   *Offers to kill her.*

 K. Edw. Hold, Richard, hold! for we have done too
  much.

 Rich. Why should she live, to fill the world with
  words? 44

 K. Edw. What! doth she swoon? use means for her
  recovery.

 Rich. Clarence, excuse me to the king, my brother;

I'll hence to London on a serious matter:

Ere ye come there, be sure to hear some news. 48

 Clar. What? what?

 Rich. Tower! the Tower!   *Exit.*

 Queen. O Ned, sweet Ned! speak to thy mother,
  boy!

Canst thou not speak? O traitors! murtherers! 52

They that stabb'd Cæsar shed no blood at all,

Did not offend, nor were not worthy blame,

If this foul deed were by, to equal it:

He was a man; this, in respect, a child; 56

And men ne'er spend their fury on a child.

What's worse than murtherer, that I may name it?

No, no, my heart will burst, an if I speak:

And I will speak, that so my heart may burst. 60

Butchers and villains! bloody cannibals!

---

39 Sprawl'st: *twitchest in death-agony*
42 Marry . . . shall: *I will, forsooth*   48 be sure: *expect*
55 equal: *compare with*   56 in respect: *compared with him*

How sweet a plant have you untimely cropp'd!
You have no children, butchers! if you had,
The thought of them would have stirr'd up remorse: 64
But if you ever chance to have a child,
Look in his youth to have him so cut off
As, deathsmen, you have rid this sweet young prince!

 K. Edw. Away with her! go, bear her hence per-
  force.   68

 Queen. Nay, never bear me hence, dispatch me here:
Here sheathe thy sword, I'll pardon thee my death.
What! wilt thou not? then, Clarence, do it thou.

 Clar. By heaven, I will not do thee so much ease. 72

 Queen. Good Clarence, do; sweet Clarence, do thou
  do it.

 Clar. Didst thou not hear me swear I would not do
  it?

 Queen. Ay, but thou usest to forswear thyself:
'Twas sin before, but now 'tis charity.   76
What! wilt thou not? Where is that devil's butcher,
Richard, hard-favour'd Richard? Richard, where art
  thou?
Thou art not here: murther is thy alms-deed;
Petitioners for blood thou ne'er put'st back.   80

 K. Edw. Away, I say! I charge ye, bear her hence.

 Queen. So come to you and yours, as to this prince!
      Exit Queen [led out forcibly].

 K. Edw. Where's Richard gone?

 Clar. To London, all in post; and, as I guess,   84
To make a bloody supper in the Tower.

 K. Edw. He's sudden if a thing comes in his head.
Now march we hence: discharge the common sort
With pay and thanks, and let's away to London   88

62 cropp'd: *broken off*   63 You have no children; *cf. n.*
64 remorse: *pity* 67 deathsmen: *executioners* rid: *made away*
75 usest: *hast the habit*   79 alms-deed: *charity*
82 come to: *befall*   87 common sort: *plain soldiery*

And see our gentle queen how well she fares;
By this, I hope, she hath a son for me.

Exit [with Clarence].

Scene Six

[London.   The Tower]

*Enter Henry the Sixth and Richard [meeting], with
the Lieutenant on the Walls.*

   Rich. Good day, my lord.   What! at your book so
  hard?
   Hen. Ay, my good lord:—my lord, I should say
  rather;
'Tis sin to flatter, 'good' was little better:
'Good Gloucester' and 'good devil' were alike,   4
And both preposterous; therefore, not 'good lord.'
   Rich. Sirrah, leave us to ourselves: we must confer.
                           [Exit Lieutenant.]
   Hen. So flies the reckless shepherd from the wolf;
So first the harmless sheep doth yield his fleece,   8
And next his throat unto the butcher's knife.
What scene of death hath Roscius now to act?
   Rich. Suspicion always haunts the guilty mind;
The thief doth fear each bush an officer.   12
   Hen. The bird that hath been limed in a bush,
With trembling wings misdoubteth every bush;
And I, the hapless male to one sweet bird,
Have now the fatal object in my eye   16
Where my poor young was lim'd, was caught, and
  kill'd.
   Rich. Why, what a peevish fool was that of Crete,
That taught his son the office of a fowl!

10 Roscius; *cf. n.*   13 limed: *caught with bird-lime*
15 male: *male parent*   18 that of Crete; *cf. n.*

And yet, for all his wings, the fool was drown'd.   20

   Hen. I, Dædalus; my poor boy, Icarus;
Thy father, Minos, that denied our course;
The sun, that sear'd the wings of my sweet boy,
Thy brother Edward, and thyself the sea,   24
Whose envious gulf did swallow up his life.
Ah! kill me with thy weapon, not with words.
My breast can better brook thy dagger's point
Than can my ears that tragic history.   28
But wherefore dost thou come? is 't for my life?

   Rich. Think'st thou I am an executioner?

   Hen. A persecutor, I am sure, thou art:
If murth'ring innocents be executing,   32
Why, then thou art an executioner.

   Rich. Thy son I kill'd for his presumption.

   Hen. Hadst thou been kill'd, when first thou didst
     presume,
Thou hadst not liv'd to kill a son of mine.   36
And thus I prophesy: that many a thousand,
Which now mistrust no parcel of my fear,
And many an old man's sigh, and many a widow's,
And many an orphan's water-standing eye,   40
Men for their sons', wives for their husbands',
And orphans for their parents' timeless death,
Shall rue the hour that ever thou wast born.
The owl shriek'd at thy birth, an evil sign;   44
The night-crow cried, aboding luckless time;
Dogs howl'd, and hideous tempest shook down trees!
The raven rook'd her on the chimney's top,
And chattering pies in dismal discords sung.   48
Thy mother felt more than a mother's pain,
And yet brought forth less than a mother's hope;

38 mistrust no parcel: *have no inkling*
40 water-standing: *flooded with tears*
42 timeless: *untimely*
45 aboding: *foreboding*
47 rook'd her: *squatted*
48 pies: *magpies*

To wit an indigested and deformed lump,
Not like the fruit of such a goodly tree.   52
Teeth hadst thou in thy head when thou wast born,
To signify thou cam'st to bite the world:
And, if the rest be true which I have heard,
Thou cam'st—   56

    Rich. I'll hear no more: die, prophet, in thy speech:
                          Stabs him.
For this, amongst the rest, was I ordain'd.

    Hen. Ay, and for much more slaughter after this. 59
O, God forgive my sins, and pardon thee!   *Dies.*

    Rich. What! will the aspiring blood of Lancaster
Sink in the ground? I thought it would have mounted.
See how my sword weeps for the poor king's death!
O, may such purple tears be always shed   64
From those that wish the downfall of our house.
If any spark of life be yet remaining,
Down, down to hell; and say I sent thee thither,
                          Stabs him again.
I, that have neither pity, love, nor fear.   68
Indeed, 'tis true, that Henry told me of;
For I have often heard my mother say
I came into the world with my legs forward.
Had I not reason, think ye, to make haste,   72
And seek their ruin that usurp'd our right?
The midwife wonder'd, and the women cried
'O! Jesus bless us, he is born with teeth.'
And so I was; which plainly signified   76
That I should snarl and bite and play the dog.
Then, since the heavens have shap'd my body so,
Let hell make crook'd my mind to answer it.
I have no brother, I am like no brother;   80
And this word 'love,' which greybeards call divine,

64 purple tears: *drops of blood*

Be resident in men like one another
And not in me: I am myself alone.
Clarence, beware; thou keep'st me from the light: 84
But I will sort a pitchy day for thee;
For I will buzz abroad such prophecies
That Edward shall be fearful of his life;
And then, to purge his fear, I'll be thy death.   88
King Henry and the prince his son are gone:
Clarence, thy turn is next, and then the rest,
Counting myself but bad till I be best.
I'll throw thy body in another room,   92
And triumph, Henry, in thy day of doom.
                         Exit [with the body].

Scene Seven

[The Same.   A Room in the Palace]

*Flourish.   Enter King, Queen [Elizabeth], Clarence,
Richard, Hastings, Nurse [with Infant], and Attendants.*

   King. Once more we sit in England's royal throne,
Repurchas'd with the blood of enemies.
What valiant foemen, like to autumn's corn,
Have we mow'd down, in tops of all their pride!   4
Three Dukes of Somerset, threefold renown'd
For hardy and undoubted champions;
Two Cliffords, as the father and the son;
And two Northumberlands: two braver men   8
Ne'er spurr'd their coursers at the trumpet's sound;
With them, the two brave bears, Warwick and Monta-
    gue,

85 sort: *find out*   pitchy: *pitch-black*   86 buzz: *whisper*
88 purge: *remove*   91 bad: *lowly*   4 in tops: *at the height*
6 undoubted: *fearless*   7 as: *to wit*

That in their chains fetter'd the kingly lion,

And made the forest tremble when they roar'd.   12

Thus have we swept suspicion from our seat,

And made our footstool of security.

Come hither, Bess, and let me kiss my boy.

Young Ned, for thee thine uncles and myself   16

Have in our armours watch'd the winter's night;

Went all afoot in summer's scalding heat,

That thou might'st repossess the crown in peace;

And of our labours thou shalt reap the gain.   20

   Rich. [*Aside.*] I'll blast his harvest, if your head
     were laid;

For yet I am not look'd on in the world.

This shoulder was ordain'd so thick to heave;

And heave it shall some weight, or break my back: 24

Work thou the way, and that shall execute.

   King. Clarence and Gloucester, love my lovely
     queen;

And kiss your princely nephew, brothers both.

   Clar. The duty that I owe unto your majesty   28

I seal upon the lips of this sweet babe.

   King. Thanks, noble Clarence; worthy brother,
     thanks.

   Rich. And that I love the tree from whence thou
     sprang'st,

Witness the loving kiss I give the fruit.   32

[*Aside.*] To say the truth, so Judas kiss'd his master,

And cried 'all hail!' when as he meant all harm.

   King. Now am I seated as my soul delights,

Having my country's peace and brothers' loves.   36

   Clar. What will your Grace have done with Mar-
     garet?

---

13 suspicion: *anxiety*   17 watch'd: *kept vigil through*
21 laid : *laid to rest, dead*
25 thou: *his brain*   that: *his arm or shoulder*

Reignier, her father, to the King of France
Hath pawn'd the Sicils and Jerusalem,
And hither have they sent it for her ransom.   40

    King. Away with her, and waft her hence to France.
And now what rests but that we spend the time
With stately triumphs, mirthful comic shows,
Such as befits the pleasure of the court?   44
Sound drums and trumpets! farewell sour annoy!
For here, I hope, begins our lasting joy.

Exeunt omnes.

40 it: *the sum raised*   43 triumphs: *public rejoicings*

FINIS

NOTES

The Third Part of Henry the Sixth. Here and elsewhere the old editions read 'Sixt' for sixth. So 'fift' for modern 'fifth.'

I. i. S. d. *Enter Plantagenet.* This is the name under which York is known in *1 Henry VI.* See that play, III. i. 163-165, and the note in this edition. It is perhaps remarkable that the *Second Part* never uses the name.

I. i. 1. *I wonder how the king escap'd our hands.* This first line, which is identical in the *True Tragedy* version, contains a violation of historic fact. The king did not escape, or attempt to escape, the Yorkists. He was found by them after the battle with a slight arrow-wound in the neck, and was treated with great outward respect.

I. i. 7-9. *Lord Clifford, and Lord Stafford, all abreast, Charg'd our main battle's front, and breaking in Were by the swords of common soldiers slain.* This account of Clifford's death is inconsistent with that given in *2 Henry VI,* V. ii., where Clifford is slain by York. Compare also line 162 of the present scene and line 47 of I. iii. The inconsistency is in all these cases carried over from the earlier plays of the *Contention* and *True Tragedy.*

I. i. 14. *brother.* The Marquis of Montague, Warwick's brother, who fell at Barnet (cf. V. ii.), was not created Lord Montague till after the battle of Towton (1461), which is dramatized in Act II of the present play. He was not York's brother, but his nephew. Has the historical Montague been merged with Faulconbridge, his uncle, who was Salisbury's brother and York's brother-in-law, and who does not appear in *3 Henry VI?* In the *True Tragedy* version Montague likewise addresses York as 'brother' at this point; but in the next scene (lines 4 and 36), where York calls him 'brother,' the *True Tragedy* has 'cosen Montague.' See notes on lines 209 and 239.

I. i. 17. *Richard hath best deserv'd of all my sons.* The precocity of Richard of Gloucester is probably the most striking of all the deviations from history in this play and its predecessor, the *Second Part.* Born at Fotheringay Castle, October 2, 1452, Richard was incapable of taking part in the first battle of St. Albans, May 22, 1455. He was less than nineteen at the time of the battle of Tewkesbury (May 4, 1471), with which this play concludes.

I. i. 32. S. d. *They go up.* The chair of state, in which York seats himself (cf. l. 51), is apparently on the upper stage.

I. i. 35. *The queen this day here holds her parliament.* The author represents these events as following immediately upon the first battle of St. Albans (May 22, 1455), but the Parliament which declared York heir to the throne did not in fact meet till October, 1460.

I. i. 47. *Dares stir a wing if Warwick shake his bells.* An allusion to falconry. Bells were attached to the legs of falcons. The best illustration I know is a passage in Nicholas Grimald's Latin play, *Christus Redivivus* (1543), II. iii.:

> 'Attamen a dominis cum dimittitur,
> Sinistra hic ales & in sublime uolitat: eam
> Adoritur atque insequitur strenuissime,
> Ac motis pendenteis tibijs campanulæ
> Tubæ sonitum supplent, crescat ut audacitas.'

'Yet, when the hawk is sent forth by its masters, it flies aloft on the left, and attacks the heron most vigorously; and, as its legs move, the hanging bells give forth the sound of a trumpet, so that the bird's daring increases.' (Translated by L. R. Merrill.)

I. i. 67. *Ah! know you not the city favours them.*
London seems to have sympathized with the Yorkists
during the entire struggle, though the citizens took no
great part in the fighting. Holinshed says, in regard
to the Queen's hostility to the Duke of York: 'She
could attempt nothing against him neere to London,
because the duke was in more estimation there than
either the king hir husband, or hir selfe.' At the
close of *2 Henry VI* (V. ii. 81) Margaret professes to
believe the reverse: 'We shall to London get, where
you are lov'd.'

I. i. 79. *Thy father was a traitor to the crown.*
The Earl of Cambridge was beheaded at South-
ampton in 1415 for plotting against the life of Henry
V. See *King Henry V*, II. ii.

I. i. 88. *And that the Lord of Westmoreland shall
maintain.* Ralph, second Earl of Westmoreland, representative of the older branch of the Nevil family,
which sided with the Lancastrians. His wife was a
daughter of Hotspur, and he a half-first-cousin of
Warwick.

I. i. 105. *Thy father was, as thou art, Duke of
York.* Not strictly true, for York inherited the duke-
dom from his uncle, the elder brother of the Earl of
Cambridge. See note on line 79 above.

I. i. 155, 156. *'tis not thy southern power, Of
Essex, Norfolk, Suffolk, nor of Kent.* Northumberland speaks as a Percy of the north. Warwick was
strong in the counties mentioned, but his power was
great also in the north, the Nevil domains being largely
in Yorkshire and Durham.

I. i. 209. *And I unto the sea from whence I came.*
The *True Tragedy* also assigns this speech to Montague, who, however, in the next scene is found at York's
castle. The words do not fit the historical Montague.
See note on line 239.

I. i. 226. *Father, you cannot disinherit me.* The

prince was born October 13, 1454, and was therefore only six years old at the time of this scene.

I. i. 239. *Stern Faulconbridge commands the narrow seas.* This line is echoed in Marlowe's *Edward II*, line 970: 'The hautie Dane commands the narrow seas.' Faulconbridge is mentioned only here in the play. He is Warwick's uncle, William Nevil, Baron Fauconberg, who commanded at Calais as Warwick's deputy in 1459-1460, led the Yorkist left wing at Towton, and was later made Earl of Kent. The special reference in the present line is to his control of Calais and the Straits of Dover during the year previous to the Parliament of 1460. There is no reason for the assumption of commentators that Fauconberg's son Thomas (also known as Faulconbridge) is referred to. The latter figures at a later period (ca. 1470) and receives much attention in the first part of Heywood's play, *King Edward IV*. I conjecture that Faulconbridge's part in the drama has been amalgamated with that of his nephew Montague, and that the figure referred to in this line is the same as the speaker of lines 14 and 209 above.

I. ii. 28-31. *And, father, do but think How sweet a thing it is to wear a crown, Within whose circuit is Elysium, And all that poets feign of bliss and joy.* These beautiful lines, which are not found in the *True Tragedy* version, reproduce very exactly the sentiment and melody of Marlowe's *Tamburlaine*. Compare lines 763-765 of that play:

'I thinke the pleasure they enioy in heauen
  Can not compare with kingly ioyes in earth,
To weare a Crowne enchac'd with pearle and golde.'

And also lines 863, 879 f.,

              'The . . . sweetnes of a crowne . . .
    That perfect blisse and sole felicitie,
    The sweet fruition of an earthly crowne.'

If the absence of such notable lines from all editions previous to the Shakespeare Folio indicates that they are additions by Shakespeare, they show how capable he was of reproducing the veritable tone of Marlowe.

I. ii. 42, 43. *In them I trust; for they are soldiers, Witty, courteous, liberal, full of spirit.* These lines also, which so praise the men of Marlowe's native Kent, first appear in the Folio. For Shakespeare's apparent interest in Kent compare notes on IV. i. 9 and IV. vii. 65, 66 of the *Second Part.*

I. ii. 47. S. d. *Enter Gabriel.* The name of the actor who represented the messenger has here been preserved. The same thing happens in the stage direction at the opening of Act III. This is good evidence that the Folio text was based on the players' copy used by the prompter. Gabriel is probably Gabriel Spencer, the actor, who was slain by Ben Jonson in a duel, September 22, 1598.

I. iii. 39. *But 'twas ere I was born.* The author has altered the relative ages of the Duke of York's sons. Edmund, Earl of Rutland, was next to Edward the heir. He was twelve years old at the time of his death and seven when the elder Clifford was killed at St. Albans. Richard of Gloucester, on the other hand, who is represented in the play as a mature warrior, was not born till 1452, and was but eight years old at the battle of Wakefield. Compare note on I. i. 17.

I. iv. 25. *The sands are number'd that makes up my life.* Modern editors usually print 'make,' but the other is a genuine plural form, characteristic of the northern English dialect. It is frequently employed by Shakespeare and other standard Elizabethan writers. For other examples in this play compare line 150 of the present scene and also II. i. 55, II. i. 83, II. v. 87, II. vi. 6, III. ii. 141, IV. ii. 3, V. v. 26, V. vii. 44.

I. iv. 33. *Phaethon.* The son of Apollo, who (ac-

cording to Ovid) attempted to guide the chariot of the
sun and was dashed to pieces.   Compare II. vi. 11-13.

I. iv. 67.   *Come, make him stand upon this molehill
here.*   'Some write that the duke was taken aliue, and
in derision caused to stand vpon a molehill.'   (Holinshed.)

I. iv. 137.   *O tiger's heart wrapp'd in a woman's
hide!*   This line, which occurs in the same form in the
True Tragedy, has been made famous by Robert
Greene's parody in his attack on Shakespeare (*Groatsworth of Wit,* 1592): 'for there is an upstart Crow,
beautified with our feathers, that with his *Tygers heart
wrapt in a Players hide,* supposes he is as well able
to bumbast out a blanke verse as the best of you: and
being an absolute *Johannes fac totum,* is in his owne
conceit the onely Shake-scene in a countrie.'

I. iv. 155.   *tigers of Hyrcania.*   Proverbially fierce
from the time that Vergil made Dido (*Æneid* iv. 367)
refer to 'Hyrcanæ . . . tigres.'   Hyrcania was a
province in ancient Persia on the Caspian Sea.

I. iv. 164.   *There, take the crown, and with the
crown my curse.*   This gesture, rather absurd in the
case of York's paper crown, is suggestive of the abdi-
cation of Marlowe's Edward II (line 2043): 'Here,
take my crowne, the life of Edward too.'

II. i. 20.   *Methinks 'tis prize enough to be his son.*
The *True Tragedy* prints 'pride' instead of 'prize,' and
the former may be the proper word.

II. i. 25.   *Dazzle mine eyes, or do I see three suns?*
The apparition here described is related by the chroniclers as occurring just before Edward's victory at
Mortimer's Cross (February 2, 1461): 'At which time
the sunne (as some write) appeared to the earle of
March like three sunnes, and suddenlie ioined alto-
gither in one. Upon which sight he tooke such courage,
that he, fiercelie setting on his enimies, put them to
flight.'   (Holinshed.)   The engagement at Morti-

mer's Cross has been omitted by the dramatist. The present scene should be imagined as occurring at Chipping Norton where Edward and Warwick met after the latter's defeat at the second battle of St. Albans, February 17, 1461, though the allusion in line 140 to 'the marches here' shows that the dramatist thought of Edward as still in the neighborhood of Mortimer's Cross on the Welsh border.

II. i. 68, 69. *Sweet Duke of York! our prop to lean upon, Now thou art gone, we have no staff, no stay!* Compare Marlowe's *Massacre at Paris,* lines 1122, 1123;

> 'Sweet Duke of Guise, our prop to leane vpon,
> Now thou art dead, heere is no stay for vs.'

The version of line 69 in the *True Tragedy* is still closer: 'Now thou art gone there is no hope for vs.'

II. i. 91, 92. *Nay, if thou be that princely eagle's bird, Show thy descent by gazing 'gainst the sun.* Alluding to the common idea, derived from Pliny, that eagles could gaze at the sun without blinking.

II. i. 113. *And very well appointed, as I thought.* This line is omitted in the Folio, probably by inadvertence. Otherwise the speech of Warwick is identical in the Folio and *True Tragedy* versions, save for a few trifling verbal alterations of the reviser.

II. i. 146. *your kind aunt, Duchess of Burgundy.* 'Isabel, daughter of John I, King of Portugal, by Philippa of Lancaster, eldest daughter of John of Gaunt: she was therefore third cousin to Edward instead of aunt.' (Rolfe.) Holinshed records that after the death of the Duke of York and his second son Rutland, 'The duches of Yorke, seeing hir husband and sonne slaine, and not knowing what should succeed of hir eldest sonnes chance, sent hir two yonger sonnes, George and Richard, ouer the sea, to the citie of Utrecht in Almaine, where they were of Philip duke of Burgognie well receiued; and so remained there, till

their brother Edward had got the crowne and gouerne-
ment of the realme.'

II. ii. 76. *Why, that's my fortune too; therefore
I'll stay.* The king was not at the battle of Towton,
but attending the Palm Sunday service at York, ten
miles away.

II. ii. 89-92. *Since when, his oath is broke; for, as
I hear, You, that are king, though he do wear the
crown, Have caus'd him, by new act of parliament, To
blot out me, and put his own son in.* These lines throw
light upon the reviser's method. In the *True Tragedy*
they are assigned to Clarence, and line 92 reads: 'To
blot *our brother* out, and put his owne son in.' In the
Folio 'our brother' is replaced by 'me,' for no obvious
reason except to reduce the length of the line; but by
inadvertence the abbreviated speaker's name, *'Cla.'*,
is left standing before line 89, and it remained for
modern editors to rectify the inconsistency.

II. ii. 144, 145. *A wisp of straw were worth a thousand crowns, To make this shameless callet know herself.* A wisp of straw was the mark of shame attached
to a scold or other female offender.

II. ii. 155. *And grac'd thy poor sire with his bridal
day.* Made a present to your father of the expenses
of the wedding. There is a gibe at the condition in
the marriage contract (*2 Henry VI*, I. i. 61) that
Margaret be 'sent over of the King of England's own
proper cost and charges, without having any dowry.'

II. iii. 1, 2. *Forspent with toil, as runners with a
race, I lay me down a little while to breathe.* The
battle of Towton lasted ten hours, on Palm Sunday,
1461; thirty thousand men were slain, and it was in all
respects the most terrible conflict of the Wars of the
Roses. The present picture of the discouragement of
the Yorkist leaders, exaggerated for dramatic pur-
poses, is suggested by a local advantage which the

Lancastrians under Clifford had gained two days before (March 26) at Ferrybridge.

II. iii. 15. *Thy brother's blood the thirsty earth hath drunk.* The 'Bastard of Salisbury,' half-brother of Warwick, was slain at Ferrybridge. It is remarkable that in the *True Tragedy* Richard announces to Warwick the death, not of his brother, but of his father Salisbury. The reviser doubtless made the correction for the sake of accuracy, since Holinshed records the historic fact that Salisbury had already been captured at Wakefield and beheaded.

II. v. 54. The latter part of this soliloquy, from line 20, corresponds to nothing in the *True Tragedy* and is a good example of the sentimental note found in many of Shakespeare's additions to the original play. There is an evident analogy to the much more mature soliloquy of Richard II on thought (*Richard II*, V. v. 1-66) and Henry IV on sleep (*2 Henry IV*, III. i. 4 ff.). It is equally evident, I think, that lines 20-54 are influenced by the style of Greene's pastoral verse.

II. v. 78 S. d. *Enter Father, bearing of his son.* The Father, whose entrance has been prepared for in the stage direction following line 54, now comes forward.

II. vi. S. d. *Enter Clifford, wounded.* The *True Tragedy* reads 'Enter Clifford wounded, with an arrow in his necke.' Clifford was actually slain, in a small engagement on the day before the battle of Towton, by an arrow in the neck.

II. vi. 8. *The common people swarm like summer flies.* This line is not in the Folio, and has been introduced from the *True Tragedy* version (cf. II. i. 113). On the other hand, line 17, which also mentions summer flies, is found only in the Folio. Both were probably not intended to remain. With these exceptions, Clifford's speech is virtually the same in the

two versions and may pass as a fair sample of the
True Tragedy style.

II. vi. 42-44. The speeches are divided as in the
True Tragedy. The Folio gives lines 42, 43, and the
first four words of 44 to Richard, Edward's speech
beginning 'And now.'

II. vi. 49. *But set.* An example of confused syntax;
'but' is redundant. Lines 47-51 are a bad example of
sentimental amplification of two simple verses in the
True Tragedy:

'Who kild our tender brother Rutland,
    And stabd our princelie father Duke of Yorke.'

II. vi. 90. *the Lady Bona.* Daughter to the Duke
of Savoy and sister to the French queen. She lived at
the court of her brother-in-law, Louis XI. Warwick
did advocate this marriage for King Edward, and was
displeased when he married Lady Grey; but the nego-
tiations concerning the Lady Bona in 1464 cannot be
regarded as the immediate cause of the open rupture
between Warwick and Edward five years later.

II. vi. 107. *Gloucester's dukedom is too ominous.*
The chroniclers comment upon the fact that three
Dukes of Gloucester before Richard had come to
miserable ends. One was Duke Humphrey, who figures
in the first and second parts of *Henry VI*, and another
Duke Thomas 'of Woodstock,' whose murder is frequently alluded to in *Richard II*.

III. i. S. d. *Enter Sinklo and Humphrey.* The
True Tragedy reads 'Enter two keepers with bow and
arrowes.' Compare note on I. ii. 47 S. d., where simi-
larly the Folio substitutes the name of the actor.
Sinklo is John Sinkler, an unimportant member of
Shakespeare's company. His name occurs in connection with small rôles in the Induction to *The Taming
of the Shrew* and in *2 Henry IV*, V. iv. (Quarto version). Humphrey seems to be Humphrey Jeffes, a

minor actor associated at different times with various companies.

III. i. 24. *Let me embrace thee, sour adversity.* The Folio reads 'Let me embrace the sower Aduersaries.'

III. ii. 6, 7. *Because in quarrel of the house of York The worthy gentleman did lose his life.* This statement, which the reviser has taken over from the *True Tragedy,* is incorrect. Sir John Grey was slain at the second battle of St. Albans, fighting on the side of Queen Margaret. In *Richard III,* I. iii. 127-130, Shakespeare gives the facts accurately, making Richard say to the Queen:

'In all which time you and your husband Grey
Were factious for the house of Lancaster.
. . . Was not your husband
In Margaret's battle at St. Albans slain?'

(In line 2 of the present passage the name of the lady's husband is given as Sir *Richard* Grey in both the *True Tragedy* and the Folio; 'Sir John Grey' is the correction of modern editors.)

III. ii. 114. *That's a day longer than a wonder lasts.* A 'nine days' wonder' being the proverbial superlative.

III. ii. 161, 162. *an unlick'd bear-whelp That carries no impression like the dam.* Fabulous natural history, reported by both Ovid and Pliny. The young bear was supposed to be born a formless mass of flesh which the mother reduced to symmetry by licking with her tongue.

III. ii. 193. *And set the murtherous Machiavel to school.* Machiavelli was born in 1469, five years later than the historical date of this scene; but the anachronism is justified by the fact that Gloucester's character owes much to the current Elizabethan distortion of Machiavelli's doctrine of the Prince.

III. iii. 16-18. *Yield not thy neck To fortune's*

*yoke, but let thy dauntless mind Still ride in triumph
over all mischance.* Lines strikingly suggestive of
Marlowe. Since they do not appear in the *True
Tragedy,* they are doubtless to be ascribed to that
poet's influence upon the reviser, not actually to his
pen. Compare note on I. ii. 28-31.

III. iii. 81, 82. *Then Warwick disannuls great
John of Gaunt, Which did subdue the greatest part of
Spain.* John of Gaunt was engaged in an indecisive
campaign in Spain in 1386-1387, and in 1367 had
served with his brother, the Black Prince, in a more
successful expedition. The theme of his rather apocryphal triumphs was apparently popular in England
during the Armada era. Kyd's *Spanish Tragedy* (ca.
1587, I. v. 48 ff.) refers to 'a valiant Englishman,

> Braue John of Gaunt, the Duke of Lancaster.
>
> .   .   .   .   .
>
> He with a puissant armie came to Spaine,
> And tooke our King of Castile prisoner.'

A book (not now extant) was licensed for publication,
May 14, 1594, under the title of 'the famous historye
of John of Gaunte, sonne to Kinge Edward the Third,
with his conquest of Spaine and marriage of his Twoo
daughters to the Kinges of Castile and Portugale, &c.'

III. iii. 95, 96. *Why, Warwick, canst thou speak
against thy liege, Whom thou obeyedst thirty and six
years.* The *True Tragedy* reads 'thirtie and eight
yeeres.' Warwick was born in 1428 and at the time
of the negotiation for the French marriage of Edward
(1464) was thirty-six years old. But the dramatists
were thinking of the general period during which
King Henry's sovereignty had been acknowledged by
the Yorkist party: i.e. from his accession in 1422 till
the final breach in 1459 or 1460.

III. iii. 101-103. *Call him my king, by whose injurious doom My elder brother, the Lord Aubrey Vere,*

Was done to death? and more than so, my father.
Holinshed reports, under date of February, 1462, that
'the earle of Oxford, far striken in age, and his sonne
and heire the lord Awbreie Veer, either through malice
of their enimies, or for that they had offended the king,
were both, with diuerse of their councellours, attainted,
and put to execution; which caused Iohn earle of
Oxford euer after to rebell.' Actually, however, the
present earl did not declare himself for the house of
Lancaster till much later (1470).

III. iii. 127. *Exempt from envy, but not from dis-*
dain. This complex sentence (lines 123-128) is taken
practically without change from the *True Tragedy.*
The idea is that Edward's love is so genuine, so solidly
rooted in appreciation of Bona's virtue and beauty,
that it need apprehend no misconstruction (*envy*),
though its very sincerity lays the king particularly
open to pain if Bona should reject his suit.

III. iii. 157. *Proud setter up and puller down of*
kings. Virtually the same words which Margaret here
applies to Warwick have been addressed by King
Edward to the deity in II. iii. 37: 'Thou setter up and
plucker down of kings.'

III. iii. 186, 187. *Did I forget that by the house of*
York My father came untimely to his death? The lines
are taken directly from the *True Tragedy,* but contain
no truth. Salisbury, Warwick's father, was captured
by the Lancastrians at the battle of Wakefield and by
them beheaded. Compare note on II. iii. 15.

III. iii. 188. *Did I let pass th' abuse done to my*
niece? The chronicles report vaguely that Warwick
had received some such injury from Edward. (Bulwer-Lytton's novel, *The Last of the Barons,* ascribes
the hostility of Warwick and Edward to abuse done
Warwick's daughter.)

III. iii. 242, 243. *I'll join mine eldest daughter and*
my joy To him forthwith in holy wedlock bands. It

was Warwick's younger daughter, Anne, who married Prince Edward, the elder having been already married to Clarence. In *Richard III,* I. i. 152, the error is corrected. Speaking of Prince Edward's widow, Richard says: 'For then I'll marry Warwick's youngest daughter.'

IV. i. 6 S. d. *Four stand on one side, and four on the other.* The king stands in the middle and the two factions group themselves at opposite sides of the stage.

IV. i. 40. *England is safe, if true within itself.* A common sentiment which forms the subject of the concluding lines of Shakespeare's *King John.*

IV. i. 47, 48. *For this one speech Lord Hastings well deserves To have the heir of the Lord Hungerford.* This passage and lines 51-55 below are based on Halle's report of a complaint against the king which Clarence made to Warwick: 'This you knowe well enough, that the heire of the Lord Scales he hath maried to his wifes brother, the heire also of the lorde Bonuile and Haryngton he hath geuen to his wifes sonne, and theire of the lorde Hungerford he hath graunted to the lorde Hastynges: thre mariages more meter for hys twoo brethren and kynne then for suche newe foundlynges as he hath bestowed theim on.'

IV. i. 70. *That I was not ignoble of descent.* Her mother, born Jacquetta of Luxemburg, was a great lady of Burgundy, who was married in 1433 to the Duke of Bedford, brother of Henry V. Upon Bedford's death she married Sir Richard Woodville, whose daughter the present queen was.

IV. i. 118. *Belike the elder; Clarence will have the younger.* Compare note on III. iii. 242, 243. Clarence had married Warwick's elder daughter, Isabel, June 11, 1469, more than a year before the marriage of his younger daughter to Prince Edward.

IV. ii. 20, 21. *With sleight and manhood stole to Rhesus' tents, And brought from thence the Thracian fatal steeds.* It had been prophesied that Troy could not be taken if the horses of Rhesus, King of Thrace, drank of the Xanthus River and grazed on the Trojan plain. The tenth book of the *Iliad* tells how Ulysses and Diomede, exponents of craft (*sleight*) and valor (*manhood*) respectively, averted the peril by slaying Rhesus on the night of his arrival and carrying off the horses. The story is referred to by both Ovid and Vergil. This allusion is an addition by the reviser of the play: lines 19-25 appear first in the Folio, whereas the rest of Warwick's speech is virtually unchanged from the *True Tragedy*.

IV. iii. 22 S. d. *French Soldiers.* This stage direction and all the business of the watchmen (lines 1-22, 26, 27) are added by the reviser. Two separate overthrows of King Edward by Warwick have been merged by the dramatists. The capture of the king here depicted took place in July, 1469, before Warwick's reconciliation with King Henry and without the aid of French soldiers. In March, 1470, Edward suddenly regained his power, and Warwick was obliged to flee to France. Here he united with the Lancastrians, and in September (1470) he landed at Dartmouth, accompanied by French troops. Edward then found himself deserted by his followers and fled to Holland.

IV. iii. 52. *Unto my brother, Archbishop of York.* George Nevil. It was in fact he who commanded the body of horse that captured Edward, July 28, 1469.

IV. iii. 53. *When I have fought with Pembroke and his fellows.* This fight took place a couple of days before Edward's capture. The Earl of Pembroke was defeated near Banbury, July 26, 1469, and beheaded at Northampton the next day.

IV. iv. In the *True Tragedy* version this scene follows the present scene five. The reviser's transposition is a dramatic improvement.

IV. iv. 2. *brother Rivers.* The queen's oldest brother, Anthony Woodville, Lord Rivers. It was he who married the heiress of Lord Scales. Cf. IV. i. 51-53.

IV. iv. 22. *blood-sucking sighs.* Alluding to an old belief that sighing exhausted the blood. See note on *2 Henry VI*, III. ii. 60, 61.

IV. iv. 31, 32. *I'll hence forthwith unto the sanctuary, To save at least the heir of Edward's right.* After Edward's flight from England to Holland, 'his wife queene Elizabeth tooke sanctuarie at Westminster, and there, in great penurie, forsaken of all hir friends, was deliuered of a faire son called Edward.' (Holinshed.) The date of the prince's birth was November, 1470.

IV. v. Two distinct events are combined in this account of Edward's escape from Warwick, as in scene three two separate overthrows of Edward by Warwick have been merged (cf. note on IV. iii. 22 S. d.). Edward's release from surveillance at Middleham Castle occurred, with Warwick's consent, in September, 1469; his precipitate flight to Holland took place just a year later, when Warwick returned to England, September, 1470, at the head of the Lancastrian forces. The stratagem by which Edward is rescued in this scene is apocryphal, but is found in the chroniclers.

IV. vi. 67. *it is young Henry, Earl of Richmond.* The future King Henry VII. He was the grandson of Katharine of France, widow of Henry V, by her second husband, Owen Tudor. The story of Henry VI's prophecy concerning the boy (who was thirteen years old at the time of this scene) is found in Holinshed. It is an evident fabrication, devised in compliment to the Tudor dynasty.

IV. vii. In the *True Tragedy* this scene and scene six are transposed. Compare note on scene four above. The arrangement of material before the reviser's changes was, then: scene iii., scene v., scene iv., scene vii., scene vi., scene viii.

IV. vii. 8. *Ravenspurgh haven.* On the coast of Yorkshire, at the mouth of the Humber River. The site is now submerged. Henry IV (Bolingbroke) landed here in 1399. The landing of Edward IV occurred on March 14, 1471.

IV. vii. 40. *Sir John Montgomery.* The name is Sir Thomas Montgomery in Holinshed, who reports that it was at Nottingham, not York, that Montgomery joined the King and persuaded him to make open claim to the crown.

IV. vii. 50. *Drummer.* Some copies of the Folio have 'Drumme,' and the *True Tragedy* 'Drum.'

IV. viii. S. d. *Exeter.* The Folio substitutes Somerset's name for Exeter's, but the latter's presence is evidenced by lines 34 ('Cousin of Exeter') and 48 ('No, Exeter'), as well as by the abbreviated name '*Exet.*' before lines 37 and 51. It is likely that the rôles of Somerset and Exeter were played by the same actor.

IV. viii. 50 S. d. *Shout within, 'A Lancaster! A Lancaster!'* Edward's troops have apparently been instructed to pass themselves off as adherents of Henry.

IV. viii. 60, 61. *The sun shines hot, and if we use delay, Cold biting winter mars our hop'd-for hay.* I.e. let us make hay while the sun shines.

V. i. 45. *You left poor Henry at the bishop's palace.* Compare IV. viii. 33, where Henry says: 'Here at the palace will I rest awhile.' Halle records that when Edward entered London, King Henry's friends fled, 'leuinge kyng Henry alone, as an hoste

that shoulde be sacrificed, in the Bishops palace of
London adioyninge to Poules churche.'

V. i. 73, 74. *Two of thy name, both Dukes of
Somerset, Have sold their lives unto the house of York.*
Edmund, the second Duke of Somerset, was killed at
the first battle of St. Albans (cf. I. i. 16). His son
Henry, the third duke, was beheaded after the battle
of Hexham, May 15, 1464. (This last battle is not
mentioned in the play.) The person addressed in the
present lines is Edmund, the fourth duke, younger
brother of Duke Henry, who was captured and beheaded after Tewkesbury (cf. V. iv.).

V. i. 81 S. d. *Taking the red rose out of his helmet.*
The revised play has no stage direction at this point,
but the *True Tragedy* inserts the following: 'Sound a
Parlie, and Richard and Clarence whispers togither,
and then Clarence takes his red Rose out of his hat,
and throwes it at Warwike.' The word 'hat' illus-
trates the fact that the actors were dressed in Elizabethan costume, not in mediæval armor as in modern
performances.

V. ii. 31. *The queen from France hath brought a
puissant power.* Queen Margaret's forces landed at
Weymouth on the very day on which the battle of
Barnet was fought, Easter Day (April 14), 1471.
Somerset made his escape from Barnet and soon joined
her. (Cf. note on V. i. 73, 74.)

V. ii. 50 S. d. *Here they bear away his body.* The
removal of the bodies of those supposedly slain was
an important detail on stages which lacked front
curtains.

V. iv. 1-38. A particularly noteworthy example of
the reviser's work. In the *True Tragedy* Margaret's
speech consists of but eleven lines, and is less resolute
as well as much less ornate. The reviser has deviated
from the chroniclers, who report that, on hearing the
news of Barnet, Margaret 'like a woman al dismaied

for feare, fell to the ground, her harte was perced with sorowe, her speache was in maner passed, all her spirites were tormented with Malencoly.' She was unwilling to risk an immediate battle, but was overruled by Somerset.

V. v. 2. *Away with Oxford to Hames Castle straight.* Oxford, who escaped from Barnet, was not at Tewkesbury and was only captured several years later (February, 1474) at St. Michael's Mount in Cornwall. He was then sent to the castle of Hanmes near Calais, where he remained in captivity for ten years.

V. v. 25. *Let Æsop fable in a winter's night.* Æsop was reported to have been a slave, dwarfish and deformed in appearance. The prince gibes at the traditional deformity of Richard.

V. v. 63. *You have no children, butchers.* On the contrary Edward had several daughters and a newlyborn son (cf. n. on IV. iv. 31, 32), and Clarence a son.

V. vi. 10. *What scene of death hath Roscius now to act?* Roscius was a famous Roman actor (died 62 B. C.) much praised by Cicero. His distinction lay in comic not tragic rôles, but his name was used proverbially by Elizabethan writers of any excellent actor.

V. vi. 18, 19. *Why, what a peevish fool was that of Crete, That taught his son the office of a fowl!* I.e. Dædalus, a fabulous contriver of marvelous mechanical inventions. Wishing to escape from Crete against the will of King Minos, he made artificial wings for himself and his son Icarus, fastening them on with wax. Dædalus made the flight in safety, but Icarus flew too near the sun, which melted the wax and caused him to fall into the Ægean.

APPENDIX A

Sources of the Play

The Third Part of *Henry VI*, like the Second Part, is based upon an earlier play, which the reviser expands largely and in an independent spirit, but without the introduction of new plot material, and apparently without further study of the historical sources (chiefly Halle or Holinshed). The sole direct source, then, of *3 Henry VI* appears to have been this basic play, *The True Tragedy of Richard Duke of York*, of which printed editions survive from the years 1595, 1600, and 1619. There is reason for inferring that the manuscript version which Shakespeare employed when he produced *3 Henry VI* gave a somewhat fuller, and perhaps otherwise more faithful, version of the original play than that found in any of the three printed editions.

The revision by which *The True Tragedy* was transformed into *3 Henry VI* was very thorough, but decidedly less thorough than that which *The First Part of the Contention* underwent in passing into *2 Henry VI*. Whereas the latter play contains about 2150 lines of new or recast matter, *3 Henry VI* contains only about 1550; and the reviser's work in *3 Henry VI* consists much more in brief casual additions or in alterations which affect the metre rather than the meaning, rather than in such long rhetorical insertions as particularly characterize *2 Henry VI*. It would appear that when Shakespeare came to rewrite the later of the two plays, he had somewhat abated the revisionary ardor that led to the elaborate poetic improvisations (often of dubious dramatic worth) with which he so generously interspersed the text of *2 Henry VI*.

The best example of the lingering in *3 Henry VI* of
the zest for rhetorical embellishment is found in the
first thirty-eight lines of V. iv (Margaret's speech),
which correspond to the following eleven lines in *The
True Tragedy*:

'Welcome to England, my louing friends of Frāce.
And welcome Summerset, and Oxford too.
Once more haue we spread our sailes abroad,
And though our tackling be almost consumde,
And Warwike as our maine mast ouerthrowne,
Yet warlike Lords raise you that sturdie post,
That beares the sailes to bring vs vnto rest,
And Ned and I as willing Pilots should
For once with carefull mindes guide on the sterne,
To beare vs through that dangerous gulfe
That heretofore hath swallowed vp our friends.'

Usually the reviser has shown more moderation.
Gloucester's famous soliloquy at the close of III. ii
(lines 124-197) has indeed been more than doubled,
but it does not dilute or misinterpret the sentiment of
the following *True Tragedy* lines out of which it has
grown:

'*Manet Gloster and speakes.*

Glo. I. Edward will vse women honourablie,
Would he were wasted marrow, bones and all,
That from his loines no issue might succeed
To hinder me from the golden time I looke for,
For I am not yet lookt on in the world.
First is there Edward, Clarence, and Henry
And his sonne, and all they (*sic*) lookt for issue
Of their loines ere I can plant my selfe,
A cold premeditation for my purpose,
What other pleasure is there in the world beside?
I will go clad my bodie in gaie ornaments,
And lull my selfe within a ladies lap,
And witch sweet Ladies with my words and lookes.

Oh monstrous man, to harbour such a thought!
Why loue did scorne me in my mothers wombe.
And for I should not deale in hir affaires,
Shee did corrupt fraile nature in the flesh,
And plaste an enuious mountaine on my backe,
Where sits deformity to mocke my bodie,
To drie mine arme vp like a withered shrimpe.
To make my legges of an vnequall size,
And am I then a man to be belou'd?
Easier for me to compasse twentie crownes.
Tut I can smile, and murder when I smile,
I crie content, to that that greeues me most.
I can adde colours to the Camelion,
And for a need change shapes with Protheus,
And set the aspiring Catalin to schoole.
Can I doe this, and cannot get the crowne?
Tush were it ten times higher, Ile put it downe.'

The finest individual scene in either version of the
play, that of the Duke of York's death (I. iv), has
been treated by the reviser with marked respect. Here
165 lines in the *True Tragedy* version are altered into
180 lines of *3 Henry VI* with only a conservative
minimum of amplification or incidental correction.

APPENDIX B

The History of the Play

The earliest allusion to any part of *3 Henry VI* is
found in Robert Greene's *Groatsworth of Wit* (1592),
where one line[1] is parodied in a connection which
shows that Shakespeare had already been employed in
revising the drama. The Shakespearean text was not
printed till the appearance of the Shakespeare Folio

[1] I. iv. 137. Cf. note on this line, p. 119.

in 1623, but the earlier play, out of which *3 Henry VI*
was produced, was published in 1595 with the title:
'The true Tragedie of Richard Duke of Yorke, and
the death of good King Henrie the Sixt, with the whole
contention betweene the two Houses Lancaster and
Yorke, as it was sundrie times acted by the Right
Honourable the Earle of Pembrooke his seruants.'
This was reprinted in 1600 and again, with some minor
corrections, in 1619. On the last occasion the *True
Tragedy* was published in combination with the early
version of *2 Henry VI* (*The First Part of the Contention*) under the blanket title of 'The Whole Contention betweene the two Famous Houses, Lancaster and
Yorke. With the Tragicall ends of the good Duke
Humfrey, Richard Duke of Yorke, and King Henrie
the sixt.' A facsimile of the title-page of the 1619 edition, which for the first time introduces the name of
Shakespeare as author, is given as frontispiece of the
present volume.

There is little evidence concerning the history of the
play in the time of Shakespeare and his contempo-
raries. The title-page of the first edition of the *True
Tragedy,* quoted above, shows that it was acted by the
Earl of Pembroke's Company of actors, who disbanded
in 1593. The Epilogue to Shakespeare's *Henry V*
(1599) implies that the Henry VI plays in general
had often been shown in Shakespeare's theatre and
had been well received. Ben Jonson's Prologue to the
revised version of *Every Man in his Humour* (1616)
refers to the plays dealing with 'York and Lancaster's
long jars' as one of the popular but faulty types of
drama of the day.

After the Restoration John Crowne rewrote *3
Henry VI* under the title of *The Miseries of Civil-War*.
Crowne's version was published in 1680, 'As it is
Acted at the Duke's Theatre By His Royal High-
nesses Servants.' The opening scenes, dealing with

Cade's rebellion and the first battle of St. Albans, are drawn from *2 Henry VI*.[1] Crowne romanticizes the story in the spirit of his age, making Warwick the unsuccessful lover of Lady Grey and adding further amatory interest by an episodic love affair between King Edward and Lady Eleanor Butler, who in the last act dons male disguisings and meets her death at Edward's hands on the battle field. Only 75 lines out of 2793 in this long piece are drawn directly from Shakespeare.[2]

That critical interest in Shakespeare's plays of Henry VI was not altogether lacking in Crowne's day appears from a note on the three plays in Gerard Langbaine's account of Shakespeare (*Account of the English Dramatic Poets*, 1691): 'These three Plays contain the whole length of this King's Reign, *viz.* Thirty Eight Years, six Weeks, and four Days. Altho' this be contrary to the strict Rules of *Dramatick Poetry;* yet it must be owned, even by Mr. *Dryden* himself, That this Picture in *Miniature*, has many Features, which excell even several of his more exact Strokes of Symmetry and Proportion.' It is probable that the Henry VI plays of Shakespeare were read more generally at this time, and with less sense of their inferiority, than in later periods.

In the next generation Theophilus Cibber produced a strange medley of Crowne's *Miseries of Civil-War* and Shakespeare's *Henry VI* under the title: 'An Historical Tragedy of the Civil Wars in the Reign of King Henry VI (Being a Sequel to the Tragedy of Humfrey Duke of Gloucester:[3] And an Introduction to the

[1] For further details of this play and of Crowne's other piece, *Henry the Sixth, or the Murder of the Duke of Glocester*, see Appendix B to *2 Henry VI* in this edition.

[2] The figures are those given by G. Krecke in his useful dissertation: *Die englischen Bühnenbearbeitungen von Shakespeares 'King Henry the Sixth,'* Rostock, 1911.

[3] I.e. Ambrose Philips' tragedy, based on *2 Henry VI*, acted February 15, 1723.

Tragical History of King Richard III). Alter'd from
Shakespear, in the Year 1720.'[1] In this work the
luxuriances of Crowne are pruned away and a large
amount of the Shakespearean text replaced.[2]

In 1795 Richard Valpy, a well-known schoolmaster
of Reading on the Thames, brought out a work entitled: '*The Roses; or King Henry the Sixth;* An Historical Tragedy Represented at Reading School, Oct.
15th, 16th, and 17th, 1795. Compiled principally
from Shakespeare.' This play opens with the an-
nouncement of York's death to his sons, Edward and
Richard (*3 Henry VI* II. i). It is essentially an
acting version, for young performers, of the last four
acts of *3 Henry VI*, with occasional borrowings from
the two earlier Parts and even, in one instance, from
Richard II. The printed text was popular enough to
reach a second edition in 1810.

A composite drama, called *Richard Duke of York,*
was made by J. H. Merivale out of the three parts of
Henry VI, and acted at Drury Lane Theatre, Decem-
ber 22, 1817, the chief part, that of York, being taken
by Edmund Kean. The greater portion of Merivale's
abridgment is drawn from *2 Henry VI,* but his fifth
act corresponds with the first act of Shakespeare's
Third Part.

The actor, Charles Kemble (1775-1854), condensed
the three parts of *Henry VI* into a single play, but
does not appear to have produced his version on the
stage.[3] In 1863 Shepherd and Anderson successfully
acted at the Surrey Theatre an adaptation of Shake-

[1] The 'Second Edition' is dated 1724; the first appeared
apparently in 1723, and the play was performed at Drury
Lane on July 5, 1723.

[2] According to Krecke (*op. cit.*) Cibber's version consists of 985 lines from Shakespeare, 507 from Crowne, and
746 of Cibber's own.

[3] The text of this abridgment was first printed, from
Kemble's manuscript, in volume ii of the *Henry Irving
Shakespeare*.

speare's *Henry VI,* entitled *The Wars of the Roses,*
the manuscript version of which was destroyed by fire
in the following year. In 1864 *3 Henry VI* (altered
and translated into German) was performed at Wei-
mar as part of a series of Shakespearean history plays
produced by Dingelstedt in honor of the poet's ter-
centenary.[1] The most important, if not the only,
recent English revival was that of the F. R. Benson
Company at the Shakespeare Memorial Festival, Strat-
ford-on-Avon, May 4, 1906. Mr. Benson himself took
the part of Richard of Gloucester.[2]

APPENDIX C

THE AUTHORSHIP OF THE PLAY

The authorship problems in the case of *3 Henry VI*
—that is, the questions, who wrote the *True Tragedy*
version, and who the altered and additional matter
found in the Folio text of *3 Henry VI?,*—are so inti-
mately associated with the similar problems presented
by *2 Henry VI* and its source, that the two Parts
cannot well be discussed separately. Reference must
therefore be made to the edition of *2 Henry VI* in this
series, Appendix C, where an attempt is made to state
general conclusions regarding the authorship of both
Parts.

In summary it may be said that *The True Tragedy*
seems to be fundamentally a work of Marlowe, though
certainly preserved in a corrupted form, while the

[1] For an account see L. Eckardt: *Shakespeare's englische
Historien auf der Weimarer Bühne,* Shakespeare Jahrbuch
i. 362-391.

[2] The entire group of history plays from *Richard II* to
Richard III was produced in sequence on this occasion.
See the London *Athenæum,* May 12, 1906.

revision represented by the 1623 text of *3 Henry VI*
is mainly, if not wholly, the work of Shakespeare in
the early years of his dramatic novitiate.

The True Tragedy, in comparison with *The First
Part of the Contention*, shows less variety of tone and
less inequality of style: it is a better unified and more
moving drama and contains fewer scenes which suggest a doubt concerning the possibility of Marlowe's
authorship.   Shakespeare's revision of this work in
3 Henry VI is, as has been already said,[1] less elaborate
and more understanding than his revision of the *Contention*. He retains better the spirit of the original and
in his alterations, extensive though they indeed are,
shows himself more the practical dramatist and less
the practicing versifier.   An advance in purposeful and
economical method appears, for example, in the reviser's rearrangement of the sequence of scenes iv-vii
of Act IV,[2] and in his occasional transposition of lines
in the original play to other positions where they are
more effective.   Line 53 of II. i, 'But Hercules himself must yield to odds,' and the opening lines of
V. iii,

> 'Thus far our fortune keeps an upward course,
> And we are grac'd with wreaths of victory,'

are found in *The True Tragedy*, but at quite different
points from those at which Shakespeare has chosen to
employ them.   Various details of the relation of the
revised to the unrevised play are discussed in the
notes; e.g., those on I. i. 14; I. ii. 28-31; II. i. 68 f.,
113; II. ii. 89-92; II. iii. 15; II. v. 54; II. vi. 8, 42-
44; III. iii. 16-18; IV. ii. 20 f.; IV. iii. 22 S.d.; IV.
vii. 50; V. i. 81 S.d.; V. iv. 1-38.

---

[1] Cf. p. 133.
[2] Cf. notes on IV. iv and IV. vii, pp. 128, 130.

APPENDIX D

THE TEXT OF THE PRESENT EDITION

The text of the present volume is, by permission of the Oxford University Press, that of the Oxford Shakespeare, edited by the late W. J. Craig. Craig's text has been carefully collated with the Shakespeare Folio of 1623, and the following deviations have been introduced:

1. The stage directions of the Folio have been restored. Necessary words and directions, omitted by the Folio, are added within square brackets.

2. Punctuation and spelling have been normalized to accord with modern English practice; e.g., warlike, afoot, sunset, Saint Albans, Tewkesbury, Phaethon (instead of war-like, a-foot, sun-set, Saint Alban's, Tewksbury, Phæthon). The words murder, murther, murder'd, murther'd, burden, burthen, etc., have not been normalized, the actual form employed by the Folio being in each case retained.

3. The following changes of text have been introduced, usually in accordance with Folio authority. The readings of the present edition precede the colon, while Craig's readings follow it.

I. i. 11	dangerous F: dangerously	
	78	It was F: 'Twas
	83	that is (that's F): and that's
ii. 38	to F: unto	
iv. 25	makes F: make	
	116	vizard-like F: visor-like
	150	passions F: passion
II. i. 55	Hews . . . fells F: Hew . . . **fell**	
	83	fires F: fire
	84	burns F: burn
	170	moe F: more
	182	march F: march amain
v. 81	an hundred F: a hundred	

87	kills F: kill
110	his F: a
124 S. d.	Alarums F: **Alarum**
vi. 2	whiles F: while
6	melts F: melt
100	in F: on

III. i. 17	thou was F: thou wast
ii. 28	Nay, then, whip me F: Nay, whip me, then
141	keeps F: keep
195	farther F: further

IV. i. 9	brother of Clarence F: brother Clarence
17	shall F: you shall
ii. 3	comes F: come
iii. 28	here is F: here's
29	parted F: parted last
v. 21	shipp'd (shipt F): ship

V. iv. 34	If case F: In case
75	my eye F: mine eyes
v. 26	sorts F: sort
27	ye F: you
50	Tower F: The Tower
78	Richard, hard-favour'd Richard F: Hard-favour'd Richard
vi. 51	indigested and F: indigest
vii. 25	that shall (that shalt F): thou shalt
44	befits F: befit

APPENDIX E

SUGGESTIONS FOR COLLATERAL READING

J. O. Halliwell: *The First Sketches of the Second and Third Parts of King Henry the Sixth* (i.e. *The First Part of the Contention* and *The True Tragedy*). London, Shakespeare Society, 1843.

A. W. Ward: *Introduction to Henry VI* in *Renaissance Shakespeare,* New York, 1907. (Reprinted in part in *Collected Papers of Sir Adolphus William Ward,* iii. 231-291, Cambridge, 1921.

C. F. Tucker Brooke: *The Authorship of the Second and Third Parts of King Henry the Sixth.* New Haven, 1912.

Thomas Heywood: *The First and Second Parts of King Edward the Fourth,* London, 1600. (Edited for the Shakespeare Society by Barron Field, London, 1842).

C. W. C. Oman: *Warwick the Kingmaker.* London, 1891.

Lawrence Stratford: *Edward the Fourth.* London, 1910.

E. Bulwer-Lytton: *The Last of the Barons.* London, 1843.

R. L. Stevenson: *The Black Arrow.* London, 1888.

Copiously annotated editions of the play have been prepared by W. J. Rolfe (New York, 1882) and by H. C. Hart (*Arden Shakespeare,* London, 1910). The edition in the *Henry Irving Shakespeare,* prepared by F. A. Marshall, also contains very full notes and a valuable introduction. That in the Bankside Shakespeare (New York, 1892) is useful because it presents on opposite pages the texts of *The Third Part of Henry VI* and of *The True Tragedy*.

INDEX OF WORDS GLOSSED

(Figures in full-faced type refer to page-numbers)

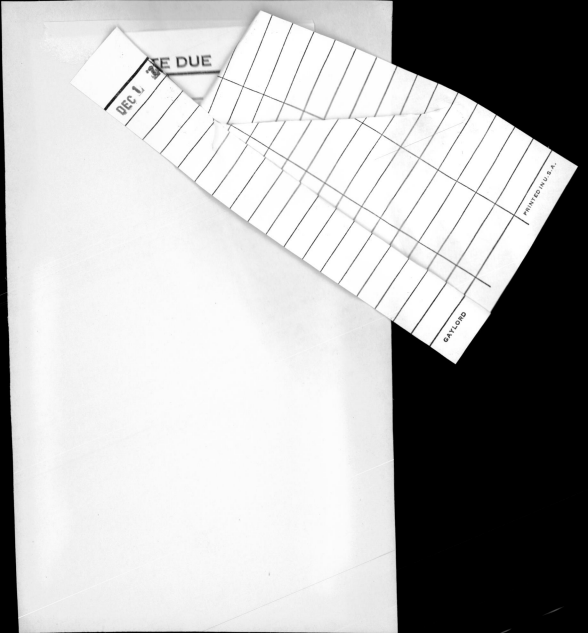